WAY

HOUSE PAINTING
INSIDE & OUT

HOUSE PAINTING

INSIDE & OUT

MARK DIXON
WITH BOB HEIDT

COVER PHOTO: **Mark Dixon**

Printed in the United States of America
10 9 8 7 6 5 4 3 2 1

A Fine Homebuilding Book

The Taunton Press, Inc., 63 South Main Street, PO Box 5506,
Newtown, CT 06470-5506
e-mail: tp@taunton.com

Library of Congress Cataloging-in-Publication Data

Dixon, Mark.
House painting inside & out / Mark Dixon.
p. cm.
"A Fine homebuilding book"—T.p. verso.
Includes index.
ISBN 1-56158-165-8
1. House painting—Amateurs' manuals. I. Title.
TT320.D57 1997
698'.1—dc21 97-13869
CIP

To my parents and teachers

ACKNOWLEDGMENTS

You can always tell who your friends are when you ask them for help with a project and they don't ask how much you plan to pay them. Those who helped with this book, and there were many, did so out of a desire to support what they viewed as a worthy effort. I would like to thank Kathy Smiley for her editorial assistance in the early stages. Les, Kristal, Cory, and Debbie also provided valuable support.

There are several painters in my community deserving of praise and thanks for sharing their expertise. Chris Passano, of Passano Painting, was nothing short of selfless with his help. (Take heed, contractors: It's not easy to escape constant pleas when you have a cell phone.) Ed Fillbach, of Bozeman Paint, was very generous with his experience and helped to review the text. I would also like to thank Mel Hirsch, another experienced painter and co-owner of The Paint Pot. Rounding out the local paint pros who contributed to this book are Jeff Keller and Glen Curry of Sherwin Williams, who generously lent their time, material, and support.

I also would like to thank everyone who allowed me to photograph and include their homes in these chapters.

Research for this book went beyond the limits of my experience. I would like to thank Gordon Rushforth, manager of architectural consultants at Imperial Chemical Industries, and Marian Cardani, PPG administrative coordinator (Coatings and Resins), for their help. The PPG Internet site greatly helped in researching new products and techniques (see Resources for the site's address).

Taunton Press deserves my heartfelt thanks for its support and encouragement. I feel honored to have Taunton as my publisher. I had the fortune of conferring with several Taunton departments, from the photographic to the editorial. My thanks go to Scott Phillips and Boyd Hagen for their photographic insights (sometimes it can only get better). A good editor is the best thing that can happen to any writer, and my editor, Ruth Hamel, is no exception. Her eye for detail and expertise brought this work to a higher level. Lastly, I cannot thank enough Julie Trelstad, the project manager, and Karen Liljedahl, editorial assistant, for their patience and support throughout this project.

CONTENTS

INTRODUCTION

Every homeowner knows that a good paint job is important, but few people know that a house's paint is the top factor used to estimate its market value. (The deck comes in third.) This certainly makes a strong argument for maintaining or improving the appearance of your house. However, my experience indicates that for most of us, an attractive home is its own reward.

When I told friends that I was writing a book on house painting, some asked me, "What's there to write about besides brushing paint on the wall?" But those who had tried getting professional results on their own knew that there was more to painting than slapping down a fresh coat of color. Choosing the right covering and applying it correctly present major challenges.

My experience with painting began as it does for many people. The exterior paint of my house was in poor shape, and I was elected head (and only) painter. Although I finished the job, I knew that if I'd been better informed about primers, scraping and sanding, and application techniques, that first project would have gone much more smoothly, and maybe would have looked better, too.

So I began to ask a lot of questions. I later went into business with a painter whose technical expertise complemented my organizational skills. He brought my painting skills up to a professional level, while I emphasized the value of thorough preparation. Together we made a good team.

As any instructor knows, a successful student is one who never stops learning. Someone close to me once said, "If I hear it, I forget it. If I see it, I remember it. If I do it, I understand it." In the years I've spent learning the trade, I've had to work hard to stay abreast of innovations. The painting business is getting more technical all the time. Just knowing the best coating to use can be a challenge. New products abound, and techniques also change.

No matter how sophisticated the painting business becomes, basic skills will always be the foundation for a top-notch job. Machines won't eliminate the need for a high-quality brush, or the importance of preparation, the most critical step in the painting process. The quality and results of any project ultimately depend on your skill and the "sweat equity" you invest in the job.

This book is designed to guide you through any painting job you undertake and to help you improve upon what you already know. In my case, finding out what I wanted to know took years of asking questions and plenty of trial and error. I'm passing along what I've learned because nobody should have to learn the hard way.

1

PREPARING A PAINT JOB

Preparation is critical to a good paint job. The extent of my preliminary work may not be obvious after the surface is covered, but poor preparation will show up very quickly in the form of failing paint.

After years in the painting business, I've learned that the preparation that goes into a project is an accurate indicator of what the final job will look like. You can see this for yourself on a smaller scale at auto body shops, which spend most of their time getting a car ready to paint.

Preparation is the foundation of a good paint job, allowing paint to look its best and last a long time. Even a minimal amount of preparation will help new paint last longer—and even the best paint can't make up for a poorly prepared job. Is the paint failing on your exterior trim or deck paint? Chances are the real culprit was an improperly sanded surface.

Technically speaking, any effort other than the actual painting can be called preparation. This includes the planning stages, inspection of the project, paint research, and of course, surface preparation. Surface preparation, or "prep," is carried out through every coat of paint, from the primer on. The good news is that each coat goes on easier, faster, and smoother than the last.

The more preparation you invest in a paint job, the better it will look. Simple as that. Remember: You may take only a few days to complete your project, but the results will be there long after you've finished.

This entire side will be sprayed, but first I have to torch, scrape, and sand (left) to blend the failing paint with the good paint and ensure an even top coat. The photo below shows how well the two portions merged.

ASSESSING A JOB

The first step of preparation is sizing up the project ahead of doing any work. One of my worst experiences was underbidding a job because I didn't foresee the "surprises" that cropped up along the way. By spending some time inspecting the surfaces you want to paint—and looking below the surface—you can save yourself trouble later.

When I bid on a new job, I'm as interested in the good paint as I am in the portions that haven't held up well, because the better portions provide the foundation for the rest of the job. Also, the paint that's in good condition shows what must be done to bring the damaged areas up to par (see the photos above). A little inspection with a scraper may reveal bare or rotted wood from moisture that has migrated through the walls—for example, near a bathroom. Or your investigation may reveal a quick-fix paint job that was put on with little care and low-grade paint.

Is there a wide gap between the way the paint looks and the way you want it to look? If so, you have a healthy-sized project on your hands. Then again, the job may only call for touching up or a fresh coat of paint. Either way, you now have a starting point for planning your project.

A friend of mine has to repaint his house every two years. It's an older house, built without a vapor barrier, and moisture makes the paint peel. My friend needs to provide a barrier and insulate the walls. The fix in this case isn't easy, but neither are biannual painting jobs.

Present paint condition

When launching painting projects, people often neglect to consider the condition of the existing finish. I recommend that you make a close inspection of the entire painting area, keeping the following questions in mind: How extensive will the project be? Is there any part of the existing finish that can serve as a match for the new finish? Is the existing finish in good enough shape to take another coat? Besides being full of surprises, this examination also will show you where to begin work.

When inspecting most paint jobs, I carry a scraper, a dusting brush, a clean rag, and sometimes a wire brush. I also use those tools to inspect the caulk, wood, trim, and substrata such as masonry.

An inspection of the exterior will turn up a wide range of conditions, from sound paint to paint that is cracked or peeling. Exposure to a wide range of temperature and moisture conditions will wear down any finish over time, no matter what the climate. The south side of the house might be weathered and peeling, while the north side only needs a good cleaning and touching up. Be sure to look for water damage from the roof or near the foundation where water might pool.

An interior inspection is the same: Search out weak areas where the paint has loosened or cracked, while also checking the paint that has held up well. Check around the windows for loosened putty, look for grease build-up in the kitchen and mildew in the baths, inspect the condition of the trim, and examine the walls and ceilings.

Even paint jobs a few years old may show signs of paint failure—areas of flaking, peeling, cracking, and blistering. Paint that's covered with layers of grime actually may be in great shape, so first lightly rub an area to see what comes off. When a good paint or stain starts to go (at an average 8.5 years, although that figure fluctuates quite a bit), it gets a dull chalk on its surface. Chalking, or slight flaking of a semi-transparent stain, tells you that it's time to recoat. If all the surfaces are chalking without more severe failure, you're actually in luck. The whole process of recoating will take less work and paint.

When assessing the paint's condition, I make a point of inspecting the surface underneath the paint. It's not enough to notice where the paint is failing; any underlying problems must be addressed. A thorough examination of the existing conditions gives you a good starting point for the painting project and keeps re-dos to a minimum (see the photo on the facing page).

PLANNING A JOB

There's more to buying paint than picking a color you like. Every housepainting project has unique features, from room size to neighborhood architecture, that should be taken into account for your home to look its best.

Design considerations

Interiors and exteriors present different design issues. When choosing colors for the inside, you should consider the rooms themselves. Do they feature lots of woodwork, or hardly any trim at all? Do you want to make a small room look larger, or vice versa? Don't forget to consider your furniture and carpeting or flooring, unless you're starting from scratch and want the furnishings to match the walls. You may want a bright kitchen and a subdued dining room. You may want to give each room a distinctive color, or you might choose one color for the whole house. Your possibilities are endless, but give them some thought.

Paint sheens present another consideration. Sheens range from flat, the least reflective sheen, through eggshell, satin and semi-gloss, to glossy, the most reflective. I recommend a high-quality flat or eggshell paint for most rooms because it's easy to maintain and touch up. A glossier finish is almost impossible to match, even with identical paint. The gloss fades over time, and not always evenly. A flat finish, on the other hand, has no sheen to fade.

Sheen can emphasize the different qualities of your rooms. Bedrooms usually look good with a "quieter" finish such as a flat or eggshell, whereas a dining room might benefit from a satin finish, which softly reflects light. Kitchens and bathrooms should be painted with a washable sheen such as a semi-gloss (flat latexes are hard to clean and tend to wash off). I've always found that a semi-gloss or satin finish sets trim off nicely. If you'd rather downplay the trim, use a flatter finish, such as eggshell. It's a good idea to stay away from glossy ceilings. They attract too much attention and tend to diminish the size of a room.

When selecting exterior colors, you need to consider wide-ranging factors, including the style and roof of the house, surrounding colors, and the climate. Start with the roof: The new color scheme should match it. I can think of a few houses that have vibrant exterior paint, but never look quite right because the color doesn't match the roof (until the roof is covered with snow).

Architectural styles also influence color choices. A Queen Anne-style house, with its many layers and patterns, will often have a shade and color for each architectural feature. In contrast, colonial styles usually have only one body color and one trim accent. But no law says you have to paint according to the style of house. You can choose to accentuate any favorite detail, whether it's your front door or another focal point.

Roof, style, brick, and stone fall into the "constant" category. Constants are the parts of the house that don't change often, and therefore are primary considerations in any color decisions. If you're seeking the advice of a paint store, I recommend taking a few photos of your house along so a color professional can better evaluate your home's constants.

Climate is a big consideration. You'll notice that region influences many color trends, such as the sharper hues used to brighten up the muted light of the Northwest. Cool pastels are better suited to the harsher light and dry terrain of the Southwest.

If you live in a country setting, the landscape may help determine the basic tones for your exterior. If you live in a city, you may be influenced by your neighbors' choices. Some neighborhood homes seem to be competitively individual in their design, while another neighborhood shares similar color schemes. What are the accent colors in your neighborhood?

Color-matching systems and state-of-the-art color computers take most of the guesswork out of what used to be a difficult process.

Whatever criteria you use in your color decisions, beware of trends. Prevailing fashions may not suit you or the region where you live. The earth tones that swept the country in the late 1970s were designed to complement the countryside, but a lot of them ended up on urban houses, where they looked dull. Paint companies' brochures often reflect the current trend. Remember that there are thousands of choices available, despite the emphasis companies place on certain hues or colors.

Narrowing your selection

Every paint store offers brochures, color chips, and color fans that feature combinations for every style and taste. Many stores have refined the selection process with programmable computers.

I've found that paint chips alone aren't enough to help me make a good choice. The manufacturers' brochures state as much, in small print at the bottom of the page, where they note that "the color of these chips may not perfectly match the paint you order." That is because most brochures use color dyes, whereas paints are colored with pigments. About 80% of the people I work with say the color they get is darker than what they expected. For this reason, I recommend going a shade lighter.

Next, try out a quart of the color you like. Far too many homeowners rush out and buy gallons of what turns out to be the wrong paint, then blame the store. There are lots of reasons that paint can appear off-color, but color mixing is seldom one of them, especially if you go to a reputable store. That's why starting with a small amount is so important. The first color you pick isn't likely to be the one you will keep, and you don't want to be stuck with custom-mixed gallons you can't use. It's not uncommon to go through 8 to 12 quarts in the search for the perfect shade. That may sound like a lot, but considering how expensive color consultants are, spending $50 to $100 for the perfect paint is a good buy. You should be able to do more than just "live" with the color you pick: You should be happy with it.

Whether you're matching an existing color or refining your selection, the process won't be complete until you've verified your choice with a "brush-out." Brush-outs let you see how the color you've selected actually looks before you invest in the total amount for the job. To do a brush-out, simply make one brush stroke from the mixed quart of paint on a wall or siding (or on a sample of that material). After the paint has dried (one hour for latex, two for oil-based paint), view it in different light and at different times of the day to see how you like it.

Brush-outs let you know if you have a color match for touch ups.

Brush-outs also are a good way to match touch-up paint. Touch-ups can be difficult because paints and stains age differently—some fade while others darken. Take a sample of the work to be matched to the paint store. Do yourself and the store a favor and take a big sample, not just a chip of the existing paint. Sometimes I'll take a window, a cabinet door, or a piece of siding. That way the newly mixed paint can be applied directly to the existing paint, blow-dried, and held up to the light for a match test.

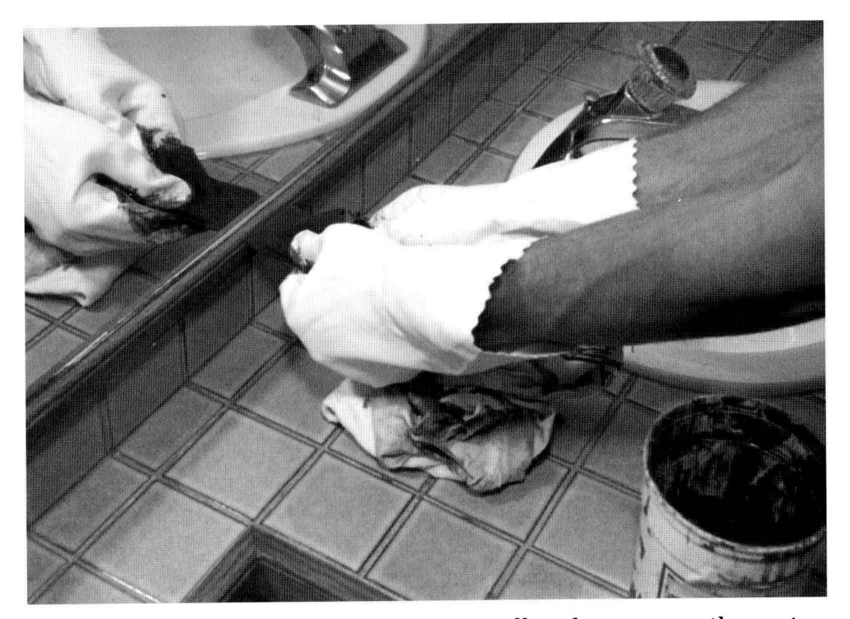

Stains are harder to match than paints. I allow for some on-the-spot mixing to ensure a perfect match.

Estimating project size

If you're planning on doing the painting yourself, your most important consideration probably will be the quantity of paint and material that you will need. The bulk of any estimate starts with measuring the total area of the paint project. To do this, you only need a tape measure, paper, and a pencil (see the photo on p. 8).

As you gain experience, you may notice other variables, such as the age and condition of the surfaces, figuring into the estimate. The more difficult estimates involve older structures that teem with "hidden agendas," or minor repairs that turn into major undertakings. Blisters on exterior siding may be caused by water evaporation from uninsulated walls. A small plaster crack may reveal large separations between lath and plaster that need to be fixed with screws and putty. The more you know about the condition of the surface and paint, the fewer surprises you'll have. Older houses can fool

You can make a pretty close area estimate with a 25-ft. tape, a pencil, and paper. Having an assistant with a calculator helps speed the process along. To get the length of the house, simply pace it off, keeping your steps close to 1 yard each.

even seasoned pros, who estimate such mystery jobs carefully and often opt for a time and material contract.

Here are some easy formulas for estimating rooms, doors, fences, and other features.

Interior estimates To determine the area of an interior job, begin with the walls. Multiply the height by the length of the sides, and add the totals. Add the ceiling area to that total. Next, figure the area of the windows and doors: If the total is 100 sq. ft. or less, don't bother deducting it from the wall area. If it's higher than 100 sq. ft., subtract that number.

The "height-times-width" formula also works for trim, doors, and windows, if you take certain variables into account. If the door has four to six panels, double its area. If it's a French door, the area should be tripled. Handrails and balustrades are estimated by multiplying the height by the length, then multiplying by four to get the total surface.

Contractors have a fast method of calculating wall and ceiling area that is almost as accurate as the process I've just described. Simply take the square footage and multiply it by 3.5 in rooms with an 8-ft. ceiling. For rooms with a 10-ft. ceiling, multiply the area by 3.75. If you're painting a new house, you can simplify your estimating by asking the drywall contractors for the total area.

Exterior estimates The methods for estimating interior surface area can be used for some exterior portions of the house, including siding, doors, windows, and handrails. However, certain architectural features have their own formulas:

For smooth blinds, use the standard "length-times-width" formula. Double the area of slatted blinds.

For plain eaves, add 50% to the total area. For eaves with rafters running through, triple the area.

Plain cornices also get the standard measurement. Triple the area if they're decorative or fancy.

For latticework, measure the area of the lattices on one side and multiply by four to get the total. Plain fences require a doubling of the area. Picket fences should be multiplied by four.

Try to make all your estimates as close as possible, then discuss them with an expert at a professional painting store. Hard and fast estimates are difficult to come by, even for professionals. If in doubt, round your figures up—it's better to have too much paint than not enough. Extra paint will come in handy for eventual repairs and touch ups. Properly sealed and stored, paint has a long shelf life. Any lumps or rust that form due to oxidation can be strained out (see p. 24).

Estimating the project time Figuring the time for a painting job is more complicated than estimating area. Contractors know that time estimates are an art that takes a while to perfect; underbidding the time factor is a major banana peel for non-professionals. A host of variables affect a time estimate, especially for older homes: the amount of set-up and preparation, structural repairs, the number of colors and coats, the types of doors and windows, and the type of surface. As the saying goes, it's all in the details. New houses and additions have fewer variables because the surfaces are new. This makes estimating the time easier.

Windows and doors can take up to 65% of the time spent painting an interior or exterior. Although I may need only a few days to mask and spray the siding or walls, I always know that the trim—notably the windows—will take another week or two. The following estimates are for one side of doors and windows, including everything from preparation to the finish coat. Bear in mind that these are professional estimates and should be used as a reference point, especially if you're new to painting. All you really need is a general idea of the time the project will take. Your focus should be quality, not speed.

Windows involve the most detail, so let's begin with them. Repainting a well-maintained window that opens (either double-hung or operating) will take about 90 minutes. Older opening windows that need extensive preparation will take twice as long. Because fixed windows are one piece, they only take half as long as windows that open. Vinyl window cladding is a low-maintenance exterior innovation. Most homes built

To calculate the area of a gabled end, turn the triangular gable into a rectangle by measuring a vertical line from the gable's peak to its bottom edge. For the horizontal line, measure the bottom edge; you now have the height and length of the rectangle. Simply halve the area for the measurement of the gable. Be sure to figure windows into your estimate.

Clad windows require very infrequent maintenance but their dense plastic is difficult to paint. Oxidized layers of plastic can be cleaned off with rubbing compound or deep-cleaning car wax.

before clad windows became popular in the 1970s have wood sashes that require much more upkeep.

A hollow-core, flat door should take from 90 minutes to two hours—about the same as a fixed window. A solid door with four to six panels will take the same amount of time as a double-hung or operating window, approximately three hours. Remember that doors also include the jambs and casing (the trim around the door). Many front doors have windows, which also add to the time.

Estimating the time it will take to paint any surface depends on how the paint will be applied. Although windows are usually brushed, doors and trim can be brushed, rolled, or sprayed, so the time required to paint them can vary.

The height of the house is an important exterior consideration. Due to the increased climbing and set-up time, a two- or three-story house takes longer to paint than a single-story house. A multistoried house also raises the question of whether to use ladder jacks or scaffolding, which take time to move and set up (see p. 42).

Time estimates are another area where a reputable paint dealer can help.

Estimating costs Your area estimate tells you approximately how much paint and materials, such as caulk and sand-paper, you will need for the job (see Chapter 3 for a complete list of materials). Every can of paint has a recommended spreading rate based on a surface that is "smooth, primed, and non-porous." Of course, not every surface fits that description. Although top coat paints generally have a recommended rate of 400 to 500 sq. ft. per gallon, I've found that most get closer to 350 sq. ft. per gallon. When estimating, it's a good idea to subtract 10% of the recommended coverage. When spraying or rolling porous surfaces like stucco, I subtract another 15%—50 sq. ft. off my adjusted spread rate of 350 sq. ft. per gallon. Again, your trusty paint dealer can help you estimate porous surfaces. Take note of the coverage you get from your paint and compare it with the manufacturer's recommended coverage.

Here's a cost estimate for a typical interior room (I haven't included an exterior estimate because the variables are simply too numerous):

A room that is 12 ft. wide, 16 ft. long, and 8 ft. high, or 630 sq. ft., with three windows and two doors, will take 4 gallons of paint. So, at $25 per gallon for a high-quality product, you can plan on spending $100 for paint. Other basic materials, such as caulk, masking tape and paper, spackle, thinner, and sandpaper, should bring the material costs to $120.

A professional would take about 16 hours to paint this room. The rates for labor range from $20 to $40 an hour, which would total $320 to $640—far more than the cost of paint and materials. According to the Buffalo (New York) Painting and Decorating Contractors of America, only 8.3% of the contractor's fee goes toward paint. The rest is overhead and labor.

Even painting one room yourself would save you enough to buy top-of-the-line brushes, rollers, and other painting tools, and still come out ahead. I know plenty of people who buy low-end equipment to "get through" their one painting project for the year, then throw everything away when the job is finished. That doesn't make much sense, since they'll eventually have to go out and buy the tools all over again. I've also found that low-end equipment gives low-end results and is depressing to work with. Professional-quality tools will give you professional results for years to come.

When you budget your paint job, don't skimp on the top coatings, whatever you do. Many homeowners mistakenly think that a middle-of-the-road paint bought at a discount chain is good enough. However, cheaper paints contain no more than 15 ingredients, compared to anywhere from 40 to 50 for top-of-the-line paints. More (and better) ingredients allow high-end paint to go on smooth and thick and dry evenly. Their coverage also is superior: One $30 gallon of paint covers as much area as two $15 gallons, to within a few cents. This means fewer coatings and less work. Lasting power alone makes quality paints a better deal. They will last, on average, two years longer on exteriors, and two to four years longer on interiors.

GALLERY OF FINE PAINT JOBS

These homes provide a wide sampling of the design considerations beneath the paint on some average and not-so-average houses.

The interior colors make the trim and wall texture the focal points of this Country French house. The trim is clear-coated to bring out the warmth of the wood, and the walls are painted a soft off-white. The owners wanted warmer tones to offset their cool climate.

The contrast of white trim against buff/beige walls had worked well on the owner's last house, making the interior more expansive than the standard combination of light walls and dark trim. When she moved to this house, she wanted something warm yet neutral to serve as a background for her artwork (left). The owner used the burnt brick as her guide to color selection for the exterior of her Tudor-style house. She softened the existing combination of white and dark brown with beige and creamy brown (above). Since the owner had a good idea of what she wanted, picking colors took only a few brush-outs.

The maintenance coating on this house required only straightforward prep: a light sanding and good cleaning, followed with a Sikkens three-part stain and sealer. The existing coat was in good shape, allowing the new coat to go on easily. Maintenance coats greatly minimize the need for major paint jobs. With regular upkeep, houses like this can go 10 years or longer before needing more extensive preparation and recoating.

A house this big requires careful color selection. The owners took their time making sure that the exterior colors blended well. They built the color scheme around the dark green, keeping an eye out for hues that would accent the house's many architectural features. Notice the small red band, which works as a subtle accent. Eight brush-outs were needed to make sure that the colors matched, but the results were worth the effort.

The house on the right is an example of regional colors used to good effect. When the owners described the colors they had in mind, the painting contractor wasn't sure it would work. But the choices turned out to be good ones. The owners wanted their house to blend with their region's natural shades, including sage (the lighter of the two greens). The white highlights accent the sage, and the strip of red ties all the colors together.

Although the colors used on this house aren't common to the region, the owners wanted to incorporate the warm pastels of the Southwest. The peach exterior sets this house apart from the surrounding houses but complements the style and attitude of the owners. The skylight bathes the kitchen with natural light, which is reflected by the washed finish of the cabinets.

This interior features several colors and moods. The rose-tinted living room above has a cool, calming feel, while the brighter peach tones of the south-facing atrium at right reflect all of the available sun.

The colors for this four-square house came from a chart selection made at the paint store. The owners wanted an older, historic color that matched the style of the house. The main color was chosen after only one brush-out. The owners came up with their own accent, a cobalt green that seems to change with the surrounding light.

The new owners of the house below were happy with the existing color scheme, so they used the same hues when they repainted. Matching tastes certainly makes color decisions easier.

These owners wanted to paint their stately house in quiet, dignified colors that would last a long time and transcend fads. The paint should last quite a while because they used a direct-to-metal primer for the wood siding and a second latex primer for the top coats.

The owners of the house below chose neutral colors that blended well with the neighborhood. As you can see, most of the larger houses shown in this section opted for subtle or neutral colors, with a few trim accents. This house is no exception. Given the house's size and high picket fence (not shown), a combination of neutral white, neutral gray, and dark-blue trim did the trick.

Although in this light the house above appears dark, its warm tones blend well with both the dark roof and the river rock in the foundation. The owners wanted a warm-colored exterior to counter the cold palette of winter.

2

PAINT AND STAIN

When you step into a paint store today, you may be surprised, and even intimidated, by the array of products on the shelves. There are primers, paints, stains, and sealers, for everything from wood to masonry—and new products are coming out all the time.

In this chapter I'll explain the differences between the products you see on the store shelves, to help you pick the right covering for your project. But first, let's talk about how paint and stain work.

Exterior stains are hardest hit by hot, dry climates. Each piece of this siding was soaked in a top-grade stain before construction, but years of exposure have dried the wood and caused the stain to flake.

WHAT PAINT AND STAINS DO

Almost every kind of surface, from drywall to concrete, needs protection from the elements. These harmful elements can range from raging blizzards to innocent-looking sunlight on a living room wall. The total thickness of the paint that ends up on the exterior of your house is usually about one-tenth the thickness of your own skin—and interior paint is even thinner. We ask a lot of that layer of skin. What it can do depends on a variety of factors, including the quality and type of paint or stain, and how well the surfaces are prepared and painted.

Paint and stain should be durable, resisting fading and abrasion, and allowing repeated washings. Interior paint should go on with minimal spattering. A quality interior stain or clear coating should resist fading, peeling, or yellowing, and also be easy to maintain, free of impurities or waxes that could collect dirt and make cleaning or recoating difficult. Exterior paints should dry with a toughness that resists deterioration from all types of exposure, and an elasticity that allows for constantly expanding and contracting surfaces. With their deep penetration and resistance to ultraviolet (UV) light, the stains and finishes on your home's exterior should provide a similar high performance.

All paints and stains degrade over time. But a good covering that isn't subjected to unusually harsh conditions will degrade slowly and uniformly.

THE HISTORY AND EVOLUTION OF PAINT

The oldest known paint was used by the cave painters of Lascaux, who ground natural pigments with water and a binder that may have been honey, starch, or gum. You may be wondering why these cave paintings have lasted thousands of years while the paint on the south side of your house is peeling after only three winters. Here's why: The constant temperature, humidity, and dark interiors of caves are ideal preservatives. Your house, on the other hand, is exposed to all kinds of weather and conditions.

The Egyptians knew as early as 1000 B.C. that paint could protect as well as decorate. Beeswax, vegetable oils, and gum arabic were heated and mixed with earth and plant dyes to paint images that have lasted thousands of years. The Egyptians used asphalt and pitch to preserve their paintings. The Romans later added white lead pigment, creating a formula that would exist almost unchanged until 1950.

The Chinese used oil from the tung tree to cement the Great Wall, and also to preserve wood. The Chinese used gums and resins to make sophisticated varnishes such as shellac, turpentine, copal, and mastic. The formulas and applications for those varnishes also changed little over the centuries.

Milk paint dates back to Egyptian times, and was widely used until the late 1800s, when oil-based paints were introduced. Odorless and non-toxic, milk paint today is being revived as an alternative interior paint. Cassein, the protein in milk, dries very flat and hard, and can be tinted with other pigments. Like stains, milk paint has to be sealed with a wax or varnish, and is very durable.

Brushes may not look like they have changed much over the years, but synthetic filaments, stronger construction, and varied styles have kept pace with the evolution of paints and stains.

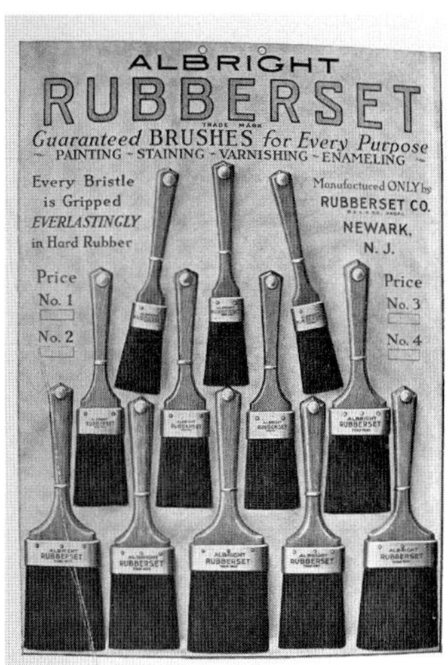

Fugi Chiseled Bristle Varnish Brushes

A very popular assortment of 12 Brushes, mounted upon a display card which makes a most attractive silent salesman.

Fashioned from hogs' bristles, badger, and goat hair, brushes also changed little for many centuries. Bristles were hand bound, rosined, and greased, then hand-laced into the stock of the brush. Hog's hair brushes, called China bristle brushes, are still a preferred brush for oil-based paints.

Pigments originally came from anything that bore a color, from ground-up Egyptian mummies to road dirt. Most mineral, or inorganic, pigments came from rust, potassium, sea salt, sulphur, alum (aluminum hydroxide), and gypsum, among others. Some extravagant projects incorporated precious stones such as lapis lazuli. Hundreds of organic pigments from plants, insects, and animals made up the rest of the painter's palette.

Paints and stains changed little from the time of the Pharaohs to the Industrial Revolution. A book on varnishes published in 1773 was reprinted 14 times until 1900, with only minor revisions. However, the colder climates of northern Europe did bring about the need for more durable paint, and in the 1500s the Dutch artist Jan van Eyck developed oil-based paint.

Starting in the Middle Ages, lead, arsenic, mercury, and various acids were used as binders and color enhancers. These and other metals made the mixing and painting process hazardous. Paints and varnishes were usually mixed on site, where a ground pigment was mixed with lead, oil, and solvents over sustained heat. The maladies that arose from toxic exposure were common among painters at least until the late 1800s, when paint companies began to batch ready-mix coatings. While exposure to toxins given off during the mixing process subsided, exposure to the harmful ingredients inherent in paints and stains didn't change much until the 1960s, when companies ceased making lead-based paints.

World War I forced the U.S. painting industry to modernize. Manufacturers had to find a replacement for the natural pigments and dyes that came from Germany. They began to synthesize dyes. Today many pigments and dyes are chemically synthesized.

Innovations in the painting industry have extended well beyond pigments. Water-based latexes have gained in popularity as a safe, quality alternative to oil-based paints. Latexes have changed from simple "whitewashes" to highly advanced coatings that can outlast oil-based products. Both oil-based and latex coatings are emerging every year with notable improvements, such as the ground metal or glass that's now added to reflect damaging UV light.

A milestone in the evolution of coatings occurred in the early 1990s with the introduction of a new class of paints and stains known as "water-bornes." Created by the need to comply with stricter regulations, water-borne coatings reduce the volatile organic compounds, or VOCs, found in standard paint and stains. Toxic and flammable, VOCs evaporate as a coating's solvent dries. They can be inhaled or absorbed through the skin, and create ozone pollution when exposed to sunlight.

THE CHEMISTRY OF PAINT

Paints and stains contain four basic types of ingredients: solvents, binders, pigments, and additives.

Solvents and binders

Solvents are the vehicle, or medium, for the ingredients in a paint or stain. They determine how fast a coating dries and how it hardens. Water and alcohol are the main solvents in latex. Oil-based solvents range from mineral spirits (thinner) to alcohols and xylene, to napthas. The solvent also contains binders, which form the "skin" when the paint dries. Binders give paint adhesion and durability. A paint's cost depends in large part upon the quality of its binder.

Because water is the vehicle in latex paint, it dries quickly, allowing for recoating the same day. The odor that you notice when using a latex paint or stain is the "flashing," or evaporation, of the binder and solvents. The binders in latex are minute, suspended beads of acrylic or vinyl acrylic that "weld" as the paint dries. Latex enamels contain a greater amount of acrylic resins for greater hardness and durability.

Alkyds and oil-based paints are basically the same thing. The word alkyd is derived from "alcid," a combination of alcohol and acid that acts as the drying agent. Both have the same binders, which may include linseed, soy, or tung oils. Oil-based and alkyd enamels may contain polyurethanes and epoxies for extra hardness. Alkyd paints come in high-performance combinations such as a two-part polyester-epoxy for industrial use and a urethane-modified alkyd for home use. Urethane boosts durability.

Water-borne coatings use a two-part drying system: Water is the drying agent, and oils form a hard-drying resin. These new coatings match and sometimes outperform their oil-based cousins. They resist yellowing, are more durable, require only water clean-up, have little odor, and are non-flammable. One disadvantage: They raise wood grain and require sanding between coats.

Pigments

Pigments are the costliest ingredient in paint. In addition to providing color, pigments also affect a paint's hiding power—its ability to cover a similar color with as few coats as possible. Titanium dioxide is the primary and most expensive ingredient in pigment. Top-quality paints not only have more titanium dioxide, but also more finely ground pigment. Inexpensive paints use coarsely ground pigment, which doesn't bind well and washes off more easily.

Additives

Additives determine how well a paint contacts, or wets, the surface. They also help paint flow, level, dry, and resist mildew. Oil is the surfactant, or wetting agent, in oil-based paint. These paints have a natural thickness and ability to flow and level; they go on smoother than latex and dry more slowly, so brush marks have more time to iron out. That's why oil-based paints tend to run on vertical surfaces more than latexes do (see the sidebar on p. 24).

Latex paint has been playing catch-up with oil-based paint over the years. Today many latexes outperform oil-based paints and primers, thanks to thickeners, wetting agents (soapy substances that are also called surfactants), drying inhibitors, defoamers, fungicides, and coalescents. Defoamers keep latex paint from bubbling and leaving pinpricks (called "pinholing") in the paint as it dries. Bubbling is caused when the soap wetting agent rises to the surface as it dries. The better the paint, the less pinholing you will have. It used to be that if latex paint was shaken at the paint store you had to let it settle for a few hours. This is no longer the case with better paints, which can be opened and used right out of the shaker with no danger of pinholing.

Coalescents help latex resins bond, especially in colder weather. Oil-based paint, because it dries slowly and resists freezing, can stick and dry in temperatures from 50°F to 120°F. With added coalescents and, believe it or not, antifreeze, some latexes can be applied in the same temperature range, and even lower. Some exterior latexes can be safely applied at temperatures as low as 35°F. Companies including Pratt & Lambert, Pittsburgh Paint, and Sherwin Williams have removed the surfactants to help their latex paints go on in lower temperatures. Because the wetting agents have been removed, the latex dries faster.

UV blocking additives have been added to paints and stains to help slow the aging process. Sunlight is responsible for much of the breakdown of any covering. It fades colors, dries paint, and adds to the expansion and contraction process that makes paint crack and peel. UV blockers in paint have consisted of finely

Special additives for flow and bonding

Penetrol gives oil-based paint better flow and wood penetration, for improved coverage. The coating will be slightly thinner, but the bond beneath will be better. You often can cut down the number of coats needed. Once my partner and I were on a job that needed to be done quickly (and right)—Penetrol allowed us to cover the trim in two coats instead of three, saving critical time.

Penetrol helps paint and stain flow easier by reducing its viscosity, or thickness, so it contacts and wets more of the surface. It's different from thinner, though. Thinner just adds more solvent, giving paint the consistency of milk. Penetrol adds penetrating oils and gives paint the consistency of half and half (light cream).

Emulsabond is the latex version of Penetrol. It turns a top coat into a primer by making it stick better to almost any material, from wood to concrete. Added to a good latex, it sticks like nothing else I've tried. However, you should only use Emulsabond in the first coat. If you use it as a top coat, it will vary the sheen, leaving a flat wall paint with glossy spots, and vice versa.

Mix Penetrol to paint before straining it to help it strain faster. Penetrol will also help any oil-based paint penetrate and flow better.

I've had great success using Emulsabond for priming "problem" surfaces such as Masonite and other dense composites, as well as older woods that need extra adhesion. Although Emulsabond makes a good primer for concrete, it will leave an uneven sheen.

A note about cleaning brushes or rollers after applying latex with Emulsabond: This sticky additive requires thorough cleaning. Start with soap and water, switch to thinner, then use soap and water again. If you only use soap and water, your brush will dry to a sticky mass.

I use Floetrol when I'm brushing latex on trim. Higher-quality latexes tend to have more body than oil-based paints. This makes them sticky, especially in warm weather. Floetrol makes it easier to coax paint into corners. It helps create an even coat, and it slows the drying time. Floetrol is especially handy for feathering long pieces of trim (see p. 51 for more information on feathering).

Oil-based paints usually need 24 hours before they're workable. Japan Drier speeds up the time it takes for oil-based paints to set, or flash, making them dry to the touch. For instance, I use Japan Drier when I'm painting entry doors that need to be closed by the end of the day. Japan Drier also comes in handy when I need the paint to set up before runs can develop. I'll also use Japan Drier to make sure paint sets before the temperature drops or a storm hits. Note: Japan Drier doesn't speed up the curing process, only the drying time.

Although all of these additives can help a job go smoother and faster, please bear in mind that you can't use them to eliminate important steps in the painting process, such as priming.

ground metals; ground glass is now being added for even greater reflection of the sun's rays.

If you live in a region with lots of humidity, rain, and insects, you may need to consider adding a biocide or fungicide to your paint. Biocide deters insects, and fungicide counters mildew. Many coatings already contain some fungicide, but only in small concentrations because of strict interstate regulations.

COATINGS FOR EVERY JOB

The right type of coating is crucial. If you pick the wrong paint, it won't matter how much time and money you spend on your project. Too many perfectly good paint jobs deteriorate too soon because the wrong primer and paint were used.

A dependable rule of thumb is to match the existing coating. If you're painting or staining over a latex, recoat with latex. You have all kinds of choices if the surface is uncoated, but you still need to consider climate, maintenance, and durability to determine the best coating for the job.

Primers

Primer is the unsung hero of any quality paint job. It determines how well the surface is protected and how long the paint will last. Knowing when to prime trips up painters almost as much as which primers to use. Basically, you need to prime when you are coating a new or bare surface; changing colors, textures, or finishes; or making a surface more uniform. About the only time you don't need to prime is when you're recoating with the same paint and finish over sound paint—for example, a flat latex over another flat latex.

To ensure compatibility, choose a product that's part of a paint system. By paint system I mean a primer and top coat manufactured by the same company. The labels of better paints always recommend specific primers and top coats for various materials and conditions. If you don't want to deal with reading the fine print, ask to see the spec, or data sheet, on a particular primer. If a spec sheet isn't available, ask to see what's known as a specifier's guide, although these guides probably have more information than you will ever need, and you might need help translating some of it.

Primers form a solid, even base for the top coats by penetrating, sealing, and bonding to all types of bare surfaces. Without first priming a new or reconditioned surface, you'll find that the top coats end up flaking off much sooner than you would expect. Even though you can use additives such as Emulsabond (see p. 24), don't make the mistake of thinking that primers are optional, or can be made out of diluted paint.

Primers even out surfaces and places that have been scraped and sanded—usually in one coat. Sometimes a surface will need a second coat of primer to ensure an even undercoat, but often one is enough. The house on p. 19 is an example of a project where two coats of primer were used. The bare wood siding was primed with an oil-based metal primer for extra adhesion, then a latex primer was applied over all the siding to give it a uniform base for the top coats. Some climates almost demand a second coat of primer. I've heard of one contractor in Florida who always double-primes to guarantee that his jobs last. If you live close to salt water, I recommend that you consider doing the same.

Primers highlight surface conditions by pointing out imperfections such as loose fibers in drywall and raised wood grain in trim. You might think that a primer would smooth a surface, but if you run your hand over a primed piece of trim it always feels rough. That's because primer forces out loose grain as it penetrates. After a dried primer has been lightly sanded, the smoothed surface is ready for the top coats. (Here's a tip: If you tint your primer the color of the top coat, you can actually speed up the painting process by reducing the number of top coats. Tinting is mostly used for color changes, although it's also handy for surfaces like bare drywall.)

Primers for interior walls and ceilings I recommend using latex primers wherever possible. Ask your paint dealer for advice on the best primer for interior trouble spots, such as the laundry room and bath, that need a good sealant and a water-resistant primer. I've always used alkyd primers in wetter areas of the house, although there are excellent latex primers that seal equally well. I prime most drywall interiors with latex, especially the bedrooms, living room, and closets. I usually spray a latex primer on new construction because new buildings have adequate vapor barriers. Also, I can paint an oil-based top coat over latex primer.

Older houses call for room-by-room decisions on what primer to use. If the house doesn't have a vapor barrier or good ventilation, you will need a primer that seals the walls and keeps moisture from getting between the surface and the paint.

Latex stain blockers and sealers may be the answer to priming damp rooms in the house. These quick-drying primers help condition surfaces with water, smoke, and tannin stains, and they can be recoated very quickly, sometimes within the hour. Pittsburgh's Seal Grip is a great latex stain blocker with few VOCs and all the advantages of an oil-based stain blocker. Quick-drying alkyd primers such as Kilz have a pigmented shellac (with high VOCs) that also acts as a stain killer and sealer, but I don't recommend these for latex top coats—the shellac might show through the latex. If your latex has what's known as good "hold out," or hiding properties, it will maintain an even sheen over primer. You can guarantee compatibility by using a high-quality latex stain blocker such as Seal Grip.

When it comes to walls, remember that plaster and drywall are different. Plaster is highly alkaline, especially when it's new, and it can leach alkaline salts if it isn't properly sealed. There are many primers you can use on plaster, depending on its condition and on the top coat and finish that you've planned.

Drywall is much less alkaline than plaster. I usually prime drywall with a latex, unless the top coats will be an oil-based paint, in which case I'll use an alkyd primer. (I know that there are perfectly good latex primers for any type of top coat, but old habits are hard to break.) When painting new drywall, I will sometimes add joint compound to the primer for a little texture. Mixed with primer, joint compound also helps smooth over any sanding marks or roughness.

Primers for interior wood When selecting primer, you should consider the nature and condition of the surface, the type of paint (alkyd, latex, or epoxy) that is planned for the top coats, and the type of finish (flat, semi-gloss, or glossy).

Most often I prime interior wood trim with an exterior alkyd primer, which seals new wood and replaces lost moisture in older wood. There are also good water-based enamel primers for interior wood. Special conditions, such as the high moisture common in bathrooms and kitchens, may call for a breathable latex primer if you can't prime all around the wood. If you can completely prime the wood before it goes up, an alkyd primer will protect most of the trim from moisture. Assess conditions like these carefully and seek the advice of a professional if your project has many different variables.

Exterior primers Even though I prefer latex paint for the exterior, I still prefer to use alkyd primers on exterior wood. They simply do a better job of priming bare wood. I'll use an alkyd primer if I know that the house has no major internal vapor problems and that the wood is in good condition (which usually means that it's new), especially if I have access to the siding and trim before it goes on. It's always best to seal all around the wood (but not the ends) to give each piece its own vapor barrier.

New redwood and cedar siding, as well as hardboard siding, needs special attention. Redwood and cedar will bleed tannins for a long time, even if the wood has air-dried for months. Before priming, you should wash out the tannin with a mild detergent, and follow this with a good rinsing. Redwood and cedar are fairly porous, so you may need to wait a day or two to let them dry. There's a good chance that more tannin resin will seep to the surface, so avoid priming with latex—the resin will bleed through. Instead, use two coats of an alkyd primer/sealer, and use a high-quality latex for the top coats. Any staining that happens after all that can usually be washed off with special wood cleaners (see the photo above).

Hardboard siding, new or already coated, presents a special challenge. The lack of grain or anything resembling a porous surface makes hardboards such as Masonite difficult to bond to. If the wood is new, pressure-wash and rinse it. If water still beads up, wash it again to remove all the wax. Seal new hardboard with a specially formulated hardboard primer/sealer, such as Pittsburgh Paints Permanizer Plus Wood Stabilizer. When mixed with a top coat, Emulsabond makes a great hardboard primer. These and other high-quality sealers also work well on aluminum or vinyl siding, plywood veneers, textured wood, and other composite sidings.

Less-toxic cleaners such as Bio-wash are good for removing stains and maintaining exterior finishes. Bio-wash is a wood cleaner that mixes with water.

Metal primers Every metal should be cleaned of oil, grease, rust, or any other residue before you prime it, so the primer gets thorough contact with the surface. Most metal surfaces can be cleaned with a good thinner. Galvanized metals sometimes come from the factory with a stabilizer that can be tough to remove, and may need more than just thinner. Check with your paint store if you want to be certain a primer will work on new galvanized metal.

There are primers for every type of metal. Ferrous metals, made of iron and steel, should be primed with a rust inhibitor. Rust is almost impossible to completely remove unless you sandblast it, and even then small pockets of rust can remain that will grow back under an unsealed surface or the wrong primer. Rust inhibitors totally seal the surface from contact with air. Some companies refer to these primers as direct-to-rust or direct-to-metal (DTM) primers. Smaller jobs like handrails can be primed with

Thanks to Sherwin Williams Direct-to-Metal primer, the paint job on this railing lasted five years with only slight fading. Here I'm applying a maintenance layer of DTM top coat that should help it last another five years.

aerosol rust inhibitors such as Pratt & Lambert's Effecto Spray Enamel, which I've had good luck using.

Other metals, including copper, aluminum, bronze, and brass, should be coated with zinc-chromate primer. Some paint companies have a specific primer for new galvanized steel. Older galvanized steel can be primed with a rust inhibitor like those mentioned above.

As with any coating, the more time the primer has to flow and contact the surface, the better the adhesion. Quick-setting primers don't flow much at all and stay right where they're painted, for better or for worse. A clean surface is especially important when you use a quick-drying primer. Note that some paint manufacturers recommend cleaning metals (and most other surfaces) with a thinner, while other companies advise against using any kind of solvent cleaner. Read the directions carefully.

An old technique that still works well for cleaning new or old metals is washing the surface with a one-to-one mix of vinegar and water. Vinegar is an all-purpose, inexpensive cleaner that will also etch a metal if mixed at that ratio. Etching metal works like sanding wood—it gives the surface "tooth" for better adhesion. That same ratio is handy for new rain gutters or uncoated aluminum siding. However, it should not be used to clean galvanized metals, because the vinegar will damage the galvanizing.

Masonry primers Whether it's inside or out, masonry usually needs a primer or sealer that will resist water and alkalis. Alkalis are salts that leach out over time, leaving a chalky stain called efflorescence. The source of the efflorescence, usually water, must be fixed for alkali-resistant primers and sealers to help. New masonry has to cure for 90 days before you can prime and paint it, especially if it is highly alkaline, like stucco.

Sherwin Williams has a masonry primer called Loxon that withstands alkalinity up to pH 13; it can be painted on masonry that is seven days old. Stucco, which is basically colored mortar and full of lime, is an ideal surface for Loxon, as is new plaster or poured concrete. (As of this printing, the jury is still out on Loxon's performance. It takes a while for a new product to pass muster in the professional ranks.) Pittsburgh Paints also has a primer for new, high-alkaline masonry, called Speedhide Alkali Resistant Primer; it's made for oil-based paint. You also can prime cured masonry with a latex top coat, but it's important that you use latex only on low-alkaline masonry. In these situations I've had good luck adding Emulsabond to the latex for extra adhesion. I recommend it for most masonry applications.

Etching with muriatic acid used to be the only way to speed up the curing time of concrete. You can still etch if you're so inclined, although if I never see another container of muriatic acid, that will be just fine. (If it etches concrete, imagine how well it etches skin!) Etching requires a bucket, hose, brush, gloves, and complete eye and skin protection. Don't forget a respirator, especially when you mix the acid to the water. Important: Add the acid to the water, not the other way around. If you add water to acid, it will splash and burn anything it contacts. And mix it in the proper ratio, usually one-to-three. Make sure you have brushes, sponges, towels, at least one 5-gallon bucket of clean water for emergencies, and another 5-gallon bucket for rinsing.

Reconditioning older, peeling concrete floors can be a chore. It's best to keep them well-maintained and recoat them regularly, before they need to be completely redone. Concrete floors in really bad shape should be sandblasted, or you can use a new system called Peel-Away that makes prepping masonry quite a bit easier (it's still no picnic). If the floor is in good shape, prep the surface and remove any trace of grease or wax with a good thinner.

For new concrete floors, I recommend a concrete stain made by H&C or Okon; they come in water-borne and silicone acrylic. My preference is the water-borne stain, since silicone is a wax that eventually will wash off. Concrete stain penetrates and seals without needing scraping or sandblasting, and resists fading better than a top coating like latex.

Older, pre-painted concrete floors have to be repainted with a similar top coating, whether latex or alkyd. A latex top coat is best applied over a standard concrete sealer, but Emulsabond also works well. An oil-based top coat requires an oil-based enamel or epoxy concrete conditioner; I would add Penetrol to the primer for a longer-lasting bond (see p. 24).

Interior paints

Did you ever wonder about the difference between interior and exterior paints? I once used exterior paint on an indoor ceiling, reasoning that it would last longer. It may last longer, but as I found out when I had to touch up the ceiling only two years later, exterior paints will discolor on an interior surface. Exterior paints contain special additives designed to withstand the outdoors. Interior paints have additives that help the paint dry to a durable, uniform finish.

Most of the advances in painting technology have been with latex. In fact, latex has overtaken oil-based paint in several areas: durability and elasticity, as well as ease of use, clean-up, and disposal. Latexes have fewer VOCs than oil-based paints. Some, such as the Pristine line made by Benjamin Moore, are made with no VOCs at all. Today's latexes are made with higher quality pigments and binders that give them more body, so they go on thicker.

Latexes enjoy quite a bit of popularity for interior applications, especially for walls and ceilings. Alkyds remain the professionals' choice for trim work because oil paints are easier to paint on detailed surfaces like molding and trim. However, that traditional school of thought is slowly changing as better latexes, including Pratt & Lambert's Accolade Interior Acrylic Semi Gloss, come on the market.

Exterior paints

Moisture is an important consideration for exterior paint selection. Each day, a family of four will generate several gallons of vaporized water inside a house. Combined with naturally occurring humidity, this can mean a lot of moisture moving through the walls and siding. Moisture is highest in the baths and kitchen. If these rooms aren't sufficiently ventilated, moisture will migrate through the walls. Vapor barriers help to contain wetness, but vapor always seeks to escape. The construction of a house, the type of vapor barrier it has, ventilation, and humidity all make selecting the right paint critical.

In wetter climates you need a paint that will let moisture pass through the wood, so water doesn't get trapped under the paint and cause blistering and peeling. Latexes are porous and let moisture pass through, unlike alkyd paints, which form a waterproof seal. Alkyds also don't flex with surfaces that expand and contract, as wood does, especially in colder climates. Latex paints have more elasticity, allowing better adhesion.

I spray with exterior latexes whenever I can because they usually hold up well outdoors.

I prefer using latex on most exterior surfaces, including wood siding, stucco, and concrete (see the photo at left). Latexes resist fading better than most oil-based paints, and they will cover either oil-based or latex primer (most oils have to go over an alkyd primer).

Latexes do a great job of covering concrete. Despite its hardness, concrete is very porous, and oil-based paints don't always stick well. For greatest durability, I recommend latex enamel.

In general, if I know of a latex product that will provide superior performance, I will choose it over an oil-based product that has to be cleaned with a thinner. Latex only requires water. Thinners add one more expense, are hard to dispose of, and usually end up spattered on my skin or clothes, no matter how careful I am (see Chapter 6 for clean-up details).

Stains

You can spend a lifetime learning about stains and sealers, but there's nothing mysterious about them. The bottom line in figuring out which stain to use is to familiarize yourself with the products available. Read the label, along with any product information you can get, and talk to the staff at a professional paint shop.

Exterior stains come in oil, varnish, polyurethane, and water-borne solvents. Stains have less colorant than paint and more solvents, giving them greater wood penetration. Waterproofing is a priority with exterior stains. Most come with built in sealants to add durability and help preserve the wood. The coloring in stains can be pigments, dyes, or both. A semi-transparent stain has more dye for grain penetration. A solid stain has more pigment for surface coating. Pigment is a finely ground coloring that doesn't penetrate the grain as deeply as a dye. That's why a pigmented stain is always accompanied by a sealer such as urethane or varnish (see the sidebar on pp. 32-33).

Some high-quality interior stains have dyes to penetrate and pigments to bring out the richness of the grain. Others contain only pigments, which are easier to apply, blend and touch up. Pigmented stains are lighter in color and bring out more of the wood grain. If you're looking for darker results, a dyed stain will provide what you want in one coat (make sure to use a conditioner on porous wood, such as pine and birchwood, to avoid splotching). Dyed stains are almost impossible to touch up. Every coating eventually will need touching up, so be sure to consider ease of maintenance in your selection of stains. You'll get the best results by using better stains such as Minwax, Pratt & Lambert's Tonetic, Pittsburgh's Rez, or Wood-Kote.

If you want to avoid the watery nature of stains, try a gel stain, which has had most of the liquid solvent removed. Gels are easy to use. They wipe on, dry fast, and cover evenly. Since they're colored with pigment, gel stains don't penetrate that well. They're a good choice for porous woods that are tough to coat evenly without a toner. Gel stains do a great job of bringing out the grain on embossed metal or composite surfaces. I don't recommend using them for hardwoods, which need a good dye stain to emphasize the depth and beauty of the grain.

Sanding sealers

Sanding sealers are interior primers that both penetrate and seal wood. You can use them under clear coats or over stains as sealers. Sanding sealers are different from a sealer like polyurethane, which is not designed to prime. They're more like varnish, but diluted with solvents to allow better penetration for priming. The hardness of varnishes and lacquers prevents them from soaking into the wood pores—sanding sealer can provide a better bond for clear coats.

Shellacs are often added to sanding sealers to strengthen the resin and provide a quick drying agent. They also add an amber tone, so if you're using a sanding sealer with shellac, make sure it won't affect the stain. Shellacs tend to yellow over time and contain toluene, which has a very high VOC content. Shellacs are slowly giving way to new sanding sealer formulas with lower VOCs and better performance.

Alkyd resin sanding sealers also have high VOCs, although less than their shellac-based cousins. Pittsburgh Paints makes a slow-drying alkyd resin sanding sealer without shellac named Rez 77-1. This particular primer/sealer is good for both interiors and exteriors. Pratt & Lambert's Latex Sanding Sealer has very low VOCs, but is strictly for interior wood and shouldn't be used under a water-borne polyurethane.

Oil-based sanding sealers also can be used to seal exterior wood, especially decking, which is constantly exposed to sun and water. For color consistency in areas like decks, it's best to completely coat, or back-prime, the wood before it goes up, using the same sealer or stain. Olympic Water Guard, Messmer's UV Plus, Behr's, and most high-end deck stains are excellent water-repellent sealers that also can be used for priming exterior wood.

Wood and stain sealers Sealers, including varnishes, lacquers, urethanes, and shellacs, are added to the stain itself, applied as a top coat over a stain, or used as a clear coat on unstained wood trim. They can be used for any type of trim, including windows, doors, and the casing around them. Although you can buy stain/sealer combinations, they tend to yellow, are difficult to maintain, and don't last as long as separately applied stain and sealers.

Varnishes contain oils such as tung oil, a very hard, durable sealant that can be brushed on and dries slowly. Varnishes are easy to clean and maintain—soap and water, followed by a wiped-on varnish, usually keeps a wood surface looking great for years. Make sure there's no wax in your cleaner, because wax clogs wood pores. I prefer to use Hope's Tung Oil varnish for a wipe-on maintenance coat. Lacquer is a fast-

This birch door has fairly even grain, so a stain conditioner isn't needed. The lamb's wool applicator in the photo on the left is ideal for stains. I let the stain penetrate the wood until I get the desired effect, then wipe off the excess with a lint-free rag (right).

Conditioners harmonize variations in grain by evenly penetrating the wood. Softwoods like pine and fir (shown here) are more likely to stain unevenly than dense woods like birch. The conditioners' solvent contains high-VOC naphtha, so use them in a well-ventilated area and take extra caution in their disposal.

When I'm working on a job where the owner is present, I have to reduce the impact of my presence as much as possible, and that includes the VOCs of the coatings I'm using. Even a low-pressure sprayer (see p. 55) would have been hard to use in this occupied interior. This is one instance where brushing was just as fast as spraying—and less hassle.

This mantel received three coats of polyurethane sealer. The third coat was ragged off 10 minutes after it was brushed on. "Ragging off" is the key to a super-smooth finish: It eliminates brush marks, fills all the pores, and doesn't allow dust to stick to the coating. Because I rag off the last coat, I don't have to wipe off the sanding dust. The dust actually helps fill the pores for a smooth surface.

Exterior wood sealed on all four sides—but not over the ends—is protected from moisture traveling through the walls, a major cause of paint problems. If the wood is only partly coated, it's much more vulnerable.

drying sealer that almost always needs to be sprayed, since it becomes tacky almost immediately.

Polyurethanes do almost everything shellac does, but they're easier to maintain. While shellacs act like paint, polyurethanes act more like a clear coat that permeates the wood instead of sitting on top of it. Polyurethanes brush on and dry quickly, with little odor and VOCs. They have more or less replaced shellacs as a clear sealer. Another reason urethanes have become such popular sealers is that they don't require sanding sealers.

The odors associated with many paints and stains can be more than just offensive—they can be toxic. Solvent-based varnishes, lacquers, and shellacs provide a super-hard coating but contain very high VOC levels. Water-borne sealers, like the stains, match the performance of many solvent-based sealers, with fewer VOCs. The VOC content of water-borne sealers such as Sherwin Williams Kem Aqua Lacquer average about 250 grams per liter, or 2 pounds per gallon, half the usual VOCs of oil-based lacquers. The ethers in water-borne sealers aren't combustible—another advantage—but they still have enough VOCs to warrant a respirator.

Although they resist yellowing, water-borne sealers such as acrylic latex polyurethanes do tend to raise the grain. They will also set up or "flash off" quickly at temperatures higher than 60°F. The best working temperature for most water-borne acrylic latex polyurethanes is between 50°F and 60°F, which lets them flash a little more slowly. In this case, flashing-off simply means that the solvent evaporates and leaves the resins to finish the drying process. A contractor I know once used a water-borne latex polyurethane sealer that flashed off so fast he could only apply it between 5 A.M. and 9 A.M. Anything later than that was too warm.

Minwax makes a very good water-borne polyurethane, as do Pittsburgh, Pratt & Lambert, Benjamin Moore, and others.

Exterior stains and sealers Because of their better penetration and sealing power, most exterior stains sold today are oil-based. However, oil-based solid stains peel as they get older, making them more difficult to maintain. A solid stain is like a paint: It coats more than it penetrates. A latex solid stain peels less and is easier to maintain as it ages. However, I prefer oil-based products for semi-transparent stains. Added oil solvents let them penetrate deeper. Some of the better stains on the market include Pittsburgh Solid Color Latex Stain, Messmer's U.V. Plus, Moorwood Solid Color Exterior Stain, Sherwin Williams Woodscape Stains, Pittsburgh Semi-transparent Exterior Stain, Rez Deck Stain by Pittsburgh, and the Sikkens Cetol system.

Deck stains usually have more solids than a typical exterior stain, which make them more durable. I recommend buying a high-end stain that is semi-transparent or what is called a trans-oxide. Until recently, the major problem with exterior stains was their low UV resistance, but newer trans-oxides have finely ground metal mixed in for greater protection. A high-end deck stain won't need a separate sealer coat, although you can add one (such as Olympic Water Guard) if you think extra protection is needed to combat moisture and sun exposure. Better deck stains retail for about $25 a gallon and cover 300 to 400 sq. ft.

Avoid using deck stains that contain silicone. Despite their low price, they are not a good deal. Advertisements for silicone stains and deck sealers often show beaded-up water on a deck, and many people are fooled into thinking that this is the sign of a successful coating. However, silicone breaks down quickly, usually in a matter of months, leaving a discolored, waxy coat that is a pain to remove. The broken-down silicone also stops repelling water.

"High-build" coatings such as Sikkens and Messmers work remarkably well on exterior siding, but they are too soft to be used on your deck. Removing these coatings takes gallons of wood cleaner and way too much work.

Water-borne exterior stains, such as Sherwin Williams Woodscapes combine advantages of oil-based and latex coatings. They run and drip less than oil stain, and dry faster, allowing for two coatings the same day. Water-borne stains have the resilience and flexibility of a latex stain, which gives them lasting power. They're a good choice for most applications. But bear in mind that cleaning up water-borne stains takes work. There are oil components in the solvent that have to be cleaned. First use soap and water, then alcohol. Ask your dealer for specific cleaning directions for water-bornes, and read the label.

The concentration of airborne VOCs is highest when paint or a solvent-based stain is sprayed. Make certain your respirator fits well and your eyes are protected.

WHEN IN DOUBT, ASK

If you still have questions about which paint or stain to use, don't hesitate to ask people in the know. An experienced, knowledgeable salesperson can clear up any questions you might have. Look for a paint store with staff who have at least 10 years of experience in the business. Ask them what has worked best for your particular application and ask to see a spec sheet on the product in question.

The answers you get will depend on whom you ask. A paint store will try to sell you one of their products—after all, that's why they're in business. Painting contractors might not be impartial, either. They need to sell their expertise. I get lots of calls from people wanting help with their painting problems. Most painters, myself included, don't mind giving an hour of our time, but if you need in-depth answers, consider hiring a contractor for a professional analysis. Rates vary, but I usually charge about $60 for a written and oral analysis, depending on the driving time involved. A paid analysis will tell you whether you should paint, stain, or re-side, as well as which coating might be best for your project. Each painting job has unique conditions that require specific answers.

3

TOOLS AND TECHNIQUES

The respirators on the left and right are ideal for all types of painting activity. The particle respirator in the middle is adequate for dust but not for vapors.

The painting industry has made tremendous strides in the last 10 years. Today there's a tool for virtually every situation. Even I'm impressed by the innovative devices coming on the market—for example, dripless caulk guns, which have solved a messy problem.

Before you begin your project, take a minute to check your equipment. You'll probably need to stock up on a few items. Make a complete list of what you need. Keep an eye out for tools that save time and labor. The more expensive equipment, such as sprayers and scaffolding, can be rented.

PROTECTIVE GEAR

Some people don't think it's necessary to wear protection when they're painting. I guess they think it's wimpy. But I've worked around enough toxic substances to understand how dangerous they can be. Dust, painting mist, and vapors affect the lungs very quickly, and skin pores are an open target for solvents and dust-borne particles. Don't be foolish—protect yourself.

Respirators

A particle mask is better than nothing at all, but it doesn't form a tight seal and it won't filter out all the dust. If you do use a particle mask, get one with double rubber bands. A damp handkerchief tied around your face gives better protection than particle masks that use lightweight rubber bands.

Double-cartridge respirators are the safest solution. They'll give you the protection you'll need for most vapors, mist, and dust. Respirators come in three sizes. Make sure that yours fits—if it doesn't fit well, it won't work well. Checking the fit of a respirator is like testing the seal of a diving mask. Breathe in, then hold your hand over the side valves. The mask fits if it presses against your face and stays there while you hold your breath. Good respirators cost from $25 on up and usually come with replacement filters. Double-cartridge respirators have color-coded filters for different contaminants; check that you have the right filter for the job. Be sure to read the instructions, and note that you should change the cartridges if breathing becomes hard or if you begin detecting vapors.

Protective clothing

Respirators do a good job of protecting your lungs, but you need to protect the rest of your body as well. Having been certified in lead abatement, I know that the body can only eliminate a very small percentage of lead, even over a 30-year span. Many painters make the mistake of thinking that a little exposure to dust or VOCs won't hurt, but it all adds up over time. I always dress for protection, keeping at least one good Tyvek painting suit on the job. Tyvek breathes well, weighs little, and provides good protection. The extra layer is a bit warm, but I would rather wear a paint suit than be covered with dust or overspray (on a hot day I make sure to drink lots of water to prevent dehydration). If you choose not to invest in a painting suit, wear clothes that you won't mind turning into something resembling a painting palette.

I almost always wear leather gloves, even when I'm brushing. They keep my hands clean and my grip dry. I carry two pairs of gloves if I'm painting more than one color, to ensure that I don't contaminate the colors. Industrial-strength rubber gloves are another must. I wear rubber gloves to stain, to wash out brushes, sprayers, and rollers; to open, mix, and strain paints; and to handle toxic substances such as paint thinners.

Rounding out my paint-anywhere wardrobe are safety glasses or goggles to keep chips, dust, and spray mist out of my eyes, and, if I'm spraying, a hood.

Respirators should be worn any time you're scraping, sanding, or spraying paint. Older paints, especially exterior paints, are likely to contain some lead. You also need to wear a respirator when working around any solvent with a high VOC content or when working with paint strippers, which contain toluene and methylene chloride.

Tyvek suits are inexpensive—about $7 each—but they do wear out. What starts out as a small back-pocket tear for the dusting brush can turn into a full-scale rip-out.

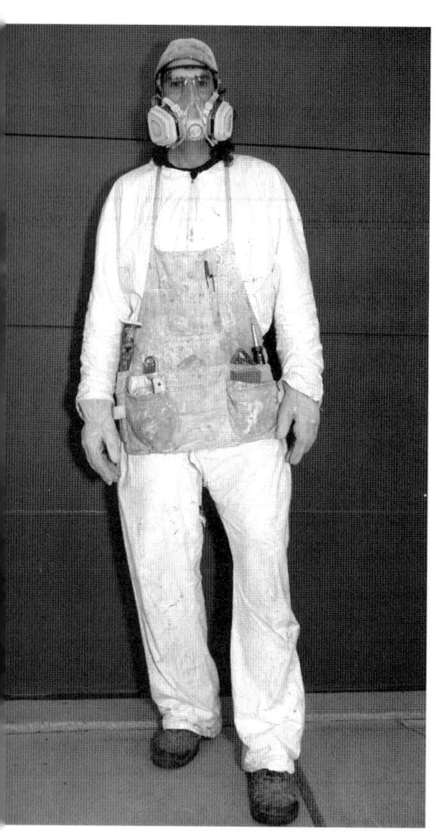

When you're dressed for spraying, there isn't much of the body that's exposed. You may look peculiar, but you'll be protected.

If you spray without a hood, be prepared to spend lots of time washing paint out of your hair.

MASKING

Usually the room you're painting will have a finished floor or carpet, and the proverbial ounce of prevention can save the day. Even if you're only painting one inside window, masking the floor is a good idea. Having an open can of paint makes me nervous if there isn't a drop cloth on the floor—I've learned the hard way. Masking becomes even more crucial if you're staining, because stain spatters everywhere. A few simple items can save you a lot of touching up, cleaning up, and struggling to get paint out of the carpet before your spouse sees it. Before I finally gave up and admitted that my technique wasn't perfectly straight and dripless, I spent more time touching up than I should have. Touching up is a fact of painting life, but these days I do much less of it because I take the time to mask.

First, you need a drop cloth. Heavy fabric is always best, but drop cloths don't have to be expensive, professional painter's cloths. You can sometimes find fairly large drapes at thrift stores, for the price of one thin plastic drop cloth. Look for drapes with vinyl backing, for added waterproofing. I pull out the top stitching for an extra 3 in. of cloth.

The trouble with plastic drop cloths is that they weigh next to nothing and billow everywhere. Plastic works best if you can find 3-ft.-wide paper (such as the kind used for flooring insulation) to lay on top of the plastic. If I'm painting a large new home and I need to mask the entire floor, the plastic/paper masking system is inexpensive and works well.

A good masking system is critical whether you're brushing, rolling, or spraying the paint. All you need is masking tape, paper for the outer edge of the floor and baseboard, and a thin layer of plastic for the windows and furniture. 3M makes a good masking system that includes special painter's tape and dispensers with pre-taped plastic. If you've ever spent hours scraping tape adhesive off windows, you can appreciate sophisticated masking tapes. Commercial masking dispensers are available at

To mask the outer edge of floors, concrete, and any large area that will benefit from protection, hold the roll of tape on your left wrist and apply the tape with the fingers of your right hand as you go along. Shorter masking pieces work best for corners and doors.

professional painting shops and sometimes at rental shops. If a commercial dispenser is hard to find, simply buy a roll of heavy paper and use your wrist to hold the masking tape (see the bottom photo on the facing page).

Some tapes need more stickiness for fixing plastic to rougher textures like walls. Other tapes need to come off without leaving adhesive on windows and smooth surfaces. Always wait at least four hours before removing tape to avoid tearing the paint. But don't leave tape on for longer than 24 hours or it will be hard to remove.

Masking floors

In addition to masking off the main areas to be painted, it's also good prevention to mask main traffic areas and wherever you plan to store and mix the paint. Distribute all the necessary drop cloths, then clean the areas you'll be taping with a vacuum, foxtail broom, or clean rag, to ensure a tight seal. As you mask, concentrate on getting a clean edge with the tape, and make sure the tape is firmly attached.

Tape and paper dispensers are ideal for masking off the outer edge of a room. They ensure a clean edge along the floor and minimize clean-up. I use shorter lengths of masking (1 ft. to 2 ft.) for corners and closets. On long, straight runs I prefer going corner to corner with one long piece of tape, which reduces the number of seams that will have to be taped. Once the perimeter is in place, I use drop cloths for the rest of the floor. For greater protection, I always substantially overlap the masked perimeter with the drop cloth. On corners I also double the cloth over to the inside, for extra protection and stability.

Getting a tight seal with a drop cloth is critical when you're spraying a room, but protecting carpet or flooring with a sealed drop cloth is a good plan even if you're just brushing or rolling. A drop cloth will move if it isn't taped in place, and you'll end up on your knees cleaning paint off the floor.

Masking walls and fixtures

No matter how you plan to apply the paint, you'll need to mask permanent fixtures such as the ceiling lights, fans, and door knobs. Even if you have excellent hand control, cutting in (edging) the fixtures that aren't masked is time-consuming, especially for multiple coats of paint. To mask fixtures, pull off enough paper and tape to wrap the fixture, being careful to keep the tape just on the base of the fixture (newspaper also makes a good masking material for fixtures). If possible, loosen the fixture covers and wall mounts to paint under them; this ensures a seamless border.

I wouldn't consider masking without a masking dispenser. This is a commercial-grade dispenser, but less-expensive home models are also available.

Setting masking tape by hand is fine if you're brushing or rolling. If you plan to spray, use a 5-in-1 or slotted screwdriver to press the edges of the tape firmly on the surface.

Fold under the corners of drop cloths to hold them in place and to prevent any overspray from getting on the floor.

To minimize the need for masking, remove as many of the fixtures as possible. Get an even line when taping the bases of fixtures, and make sure the tape is well sealed.

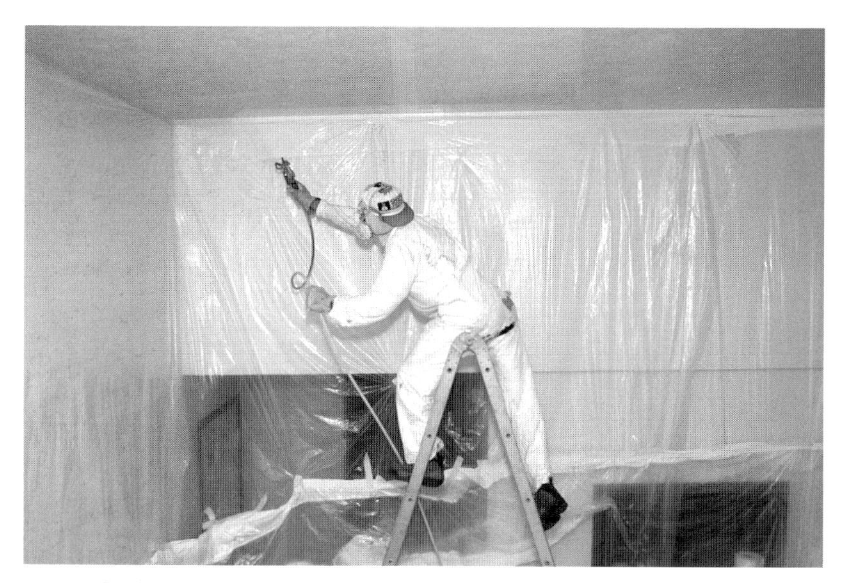

To mask walls, go around the room horizontally with 1½-in. masking tape, leaving half the tape's width free to stick to the plastic. If your walls are higher than your plastic, simply go around the room again with another length and tape it to the bottom of the first band. Test a strip of the tape on the wall to make sure it won't pull the paint off.

The amount of masking that you should do depends on what kind of painting you'll be doing. The only time the walls need to be masked is when you plan to spray the ceiling and you need to keep the walls dry—for instance, if the ceiling is getting a different color or finish. If the trim is clear-coated or you intend to paint only the walls and ceiling, it's wise to mask all around the trim, especially the windowsills.

Masking windows

The only time I mask windows is when I plan to spray. Taping windows isn't very effective. It takes too long, paint still gets under the tape, and masking tape has a knack for really sticking to glass.

For interior or exterior windows, I use the same system as for masking walls (see the bottom photo at left). The only difference is that masking windows usually is faster than masking whole walls. Masking windows and walls is usually

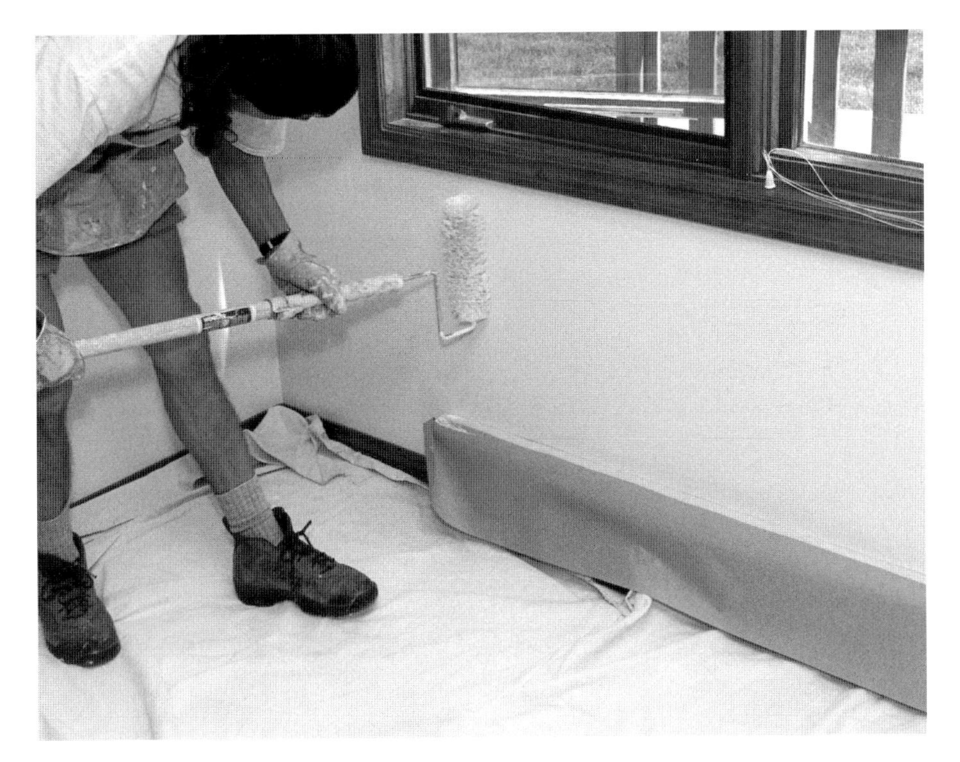

To protect windows when I'm rolling walls, I sometimes put masking paper over the top edge of the window casing. I use this same technique to mask the floor base and molding. Here I've covered the baseboard with masking paper. If you're using a high-quality paint and roller cover, which minimize spatter, you probably can use wide masking tape instead of masking paper over the top window sash.

done with plastic, which lets light into the room and is handy for covering large areas (paper is best for masking floors and trim). To measure plastic, I roll it out along the window, cut as straight a line as possible, and tape the perimeter of the window. Then it's simply a matter of sticking the plastic onto the exposed tape, working from the top down and being careful to keep it straight and level.

Masking paper also works well to protect windows, floor base, and molding from paint spatters. To protect windows, apply masking paper over the top edge of the window casing. The width of the paper is enough to block most of the roller spatter. This same technique protects the floor base and molding. If you're confident about your brushing and rolling abilities, try using 1½-in. masking tape instead of masking paper.

Extra-long roller nap and quality paint let me get away with using 1½-in. masking tape as a spatter shield on the trim. Anyone can use this method if you take extra care with your brushwork and use high-end equipment and paint.

Masking for spraying

Spraying demands that anything *not* being sprayed should be completely masked. Because spraying requires such extensive masking, wait to mask until you're ready to spray. Exterior spraying might require extensive masking, depending on the number of colors and whether there are surrounding structures such as fences and power lines. When masking for spray, remember to be thorough. Overspray is hard to control, especially under windy conditions. The more you've prepared for overspray, the better. The time spent masking is much less than the time you would have spent touching up afterward. A tight seal with masking tape is critical because sprayed paint gets everywhere. Overspray is like the occasional drip from a brush—every so often one will get away from you, no matter how careful you are. But you can minimize overspray by double-checking before you spray.

I use a paper dispenser to wrap gutters, wires, and the bases of buildings, as well as longer runs that need masking, such as trim and the undersides of eaves.

LADDERS AND SCAFFOLDING

Most of a painting job calls for constant movement from one end of wall to the other, as when you're rolling or spraying. Constant movement means a lot of climbing up and down and repositioning, so it's best to keep your equipment light and portable.

Ladders and accessories

Like paints, ladders have evolved greatly over the last 20 years. The strength and lightness of aluminum and fiberglass have improved ladder safety. Extension ladders now feature innovations including pivoting rubber feet, base extensions for leveling, and wall extensions for better overhead access. A good aluminum alloy makes the strongest and lightest ladder. Fiberglass is heavier than aluminum and almost as strong, and can have the added advantage of being non-conductive (though a non-conductive ladder costs more). Considering how many electrical accidents happen with ladders, a non-conductive ladder probably is worth the investment. Wood ladders are heavier than either aluminum or fiberglass, but their lower cost and stability keep them popular. Not everyone likes the bouncy feel of a wood ladder, but they do have wider treads, and as far as I'm concerned, the flatter the step, the better. When choosing a ladder, always check to see that the rungs are flattened on the top. You'll notice that better commercial and industrial ladders come with flattened rungs and extra support braces.

The ladder I use most often for painting interiors is a 2-ft. aluminum stepladder made by Werner. This ladder is 30 in. wide instead of the usual 12 in., giving you a more stable platform. Painting on top of a standard 2-ft. stepladder isn't very stable. There's nothing to brace against, and it's easier than you might think to fall. In fact, the only time I've ever fallen was off a 2-ft. stepladder, directly into a pile of tools and buckets.

My all-around ladder is a versatile stepladder/extension ladder combination made by Little Giant. These ladders are versatile and solid. The Little Giant has equally weighted legs for greater stability, compared to a typical 6-ft. stepladder with lighter front legs. I have to say I prefer carrying two Little Giants around to hauling two standard stepladders and two extension ladders. Although I use the Little Giants for almost every job, some projects call for longer extension ladders. Remember: Most ladders can be rented.

If I could only use two ladders for the rest of my life, I'd pick these. The Little Giant (in back) is a versatile stepladder/extension ladder, stretching from 5½ to 22 ft. The 2-ft. Werner ladder has a sturdy 30-in. base that lets me work off both sides without tipping.

Ladder accessories include base extensions to level the ladder on uneven ground, top extensions, foam ladder mitts that protect walls and siding, wood blocks that act as extra leveling shims (I always have an assortment of wood pieces that are at least 8 in. square), a swivel hook for the paint can, a foot platform, and knee pads.

An uncushioned ladder will mar the surface of a wall or exterior siding. I layer soft rags and tape them together about 6 in. from the ladder end. Ladder mitts also work well, but they can become hard and brittle under a build-up of spray and finish. So if you use them, keep them clean.

Ladder work doesn't have to be uncomfortable. Standing for very long on ladder rungs, especially round ones, is hard on the feet. Foot platforms take the weight off the 2-in. part of your foot that contacts the rung, making standing much easier. The taller you are, the more weight you have to brace with your knees. I highly recommend using knee pads for working on extension ladders. Construction-style knee pads aren't ideal for standing, but athletic knee pads work great.

Scaffolding and ladder jacks

Two ladders, one sturdy plank, and two ladder jacks: These are the basics for a scaffolding system, and they're all rentable. If you rent, be sure that everything is in good working order and that you understand how to set it up. Whenever I rent extra scaffolding, I

This shows two types of extension ladders, ladder jacks, and a plank. Notice that because the ladders are set at different angles, the ladder jacks go in opposite directions one to the inside, the other to the outside. The plank is level and parallel to the side of the house. The ladder bases are braced and level. These planks cost about $200 new, but I was able to make this setup for quite a bit less using scrap aluminum, plywood, and rivets.

make sure I have some spray lubricant in case I need to free up some rusted connections. Make sure that the plank is in good shape and not warped, since that's where you'll be spending most of your time.

Planks need to be 1 ft. wide and sturdy. A good plank should easily hold two people and their gear. Whatever material you use should be strong and light; aluminum-plywood planking is best. Avoid using wood planks, which will warp, crack, and break over time. Wood planking is also heavy and difficult to move. If you do want to use wood, keep the planks 10 ft. or less.

The better ladder jacks, like those made by Werner, have three rung supports and a locking pin to keep the jack from coming off. Ladder jacks with two rung supports work fine, though, and are sometimes easier to fit on a ladder. Newer ladder jacks also come with plank clamps, a valuable safety feature.

Pump jacks use 4x4s (or two 2x4s nailed together) for risers and have a foot pedal to raise and lower the plank. Frankly, I don't recommend them. It's dangerous to put your life and faith in a couple of long, wobbly 4x4s. If you have pump jacks, do yourself a favor and retire them.

Safety

The motto "safety first" should really be "safety first, during, and last." It's critical to place ladders and scaffolding on solid footing, at a 75-degree angle. If the ground is damp or soft, try jumping on the first ladder rung a few times to plant the feet firmly in the earth. Wear a work belt or painting apron so one of your hands is free.

Be aware of where your feet are when working above ground, and make your movements slow and deliberate. Take a break as soon as you feel tired. It takes a while to get completely comfortable working on ladders and scaffolding, so go easy until you feel more relaxed. Remember that a little bounce or flex is normal; if ladders were rigid they wouldn't last long.

Whatever system you choose for scaffolding, never use a nailed-together, inverted "L" or "V" frame against the

Most homes have 8-ft. interior ceilings; for these I only need a 2-ft. stepladder. If I'm working inside a house with high ceilings, one Little Giant is all I need to reach most peaks. It extends high enough that I can keep my balance even with the ladder fully extended, and it's easy to move around the room.

side of a house. These kinds of scaffolds are unstable and wobbly—accidents waiting to happen.

Although scaffolding is used mostly for exterior painting, I use it for inside jobs when I'm working in high areas for a long time. In general, though, I try to keep ladders and scaffolding to a minimum for both interior and exterior painting. The less there is to haul, move around, and set up, the better.

Roof jacks are necessary when there are gables to be painted. You can buy or rent construction roof jacks that attach directly to the roof and work reasonably well. Since I have my own planks, I prefer to make wood braces to fit the pitch. It's a simple system: I cut lengths of steel banding and attach it to the bottom of each brace, then nail the extended length of banding to the roof. (It's best to use rubber washers with the nails and to use the same nails to fill the holes after you remove the roof jacks.) The banding is used by lumber yards for shipping; they usually throw it away, but it's perfect for securing roof jacks.

These "customized" roof jacks take longer to set up than a fixed-angle jack, but they're more secure. I cut out three braces (jacks) for each plank and nail banding on the bottom of each brace, keeping the lengths of banding the same. This is a two-person job—doing it solo requires lots of caution. Once the planking is on, check for contact along the braces, and secure the plank to the braces.

If a scraper is sharp, you shouldn't have to exert much energy. Here I'm pulling off an oxidized clear coat and getting down to an intact layer. After scraping, smooth the surface with sandpaper.

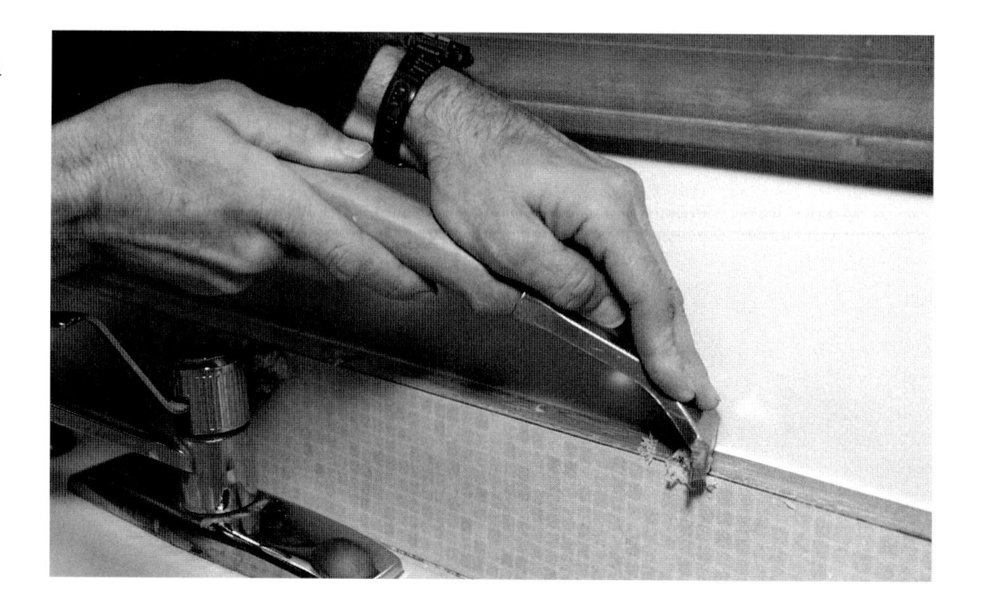

SCRAPERS

The scraper is the first tool I use for preparation, to knock off as much of the peeling and blistering paint as I can. I work with two types of scrapers: a box scraper with multiple edges for flat surfaces, and a shave-hook for rounded and grooved surfaces. The box scraper is a common item in paint stores, but a shave-hook is a specialty scraper that you'll most likely find in woodworking stores (I get mine through a mail-order woodworking catalog). Sharp scrapers keep the job moving fast, so be prepared to change or sharpen blades more than once during the job, especially if the project is outside. Outside paint takes more of a beating than interior paint, and requires more scraping.

Like everything else in the painting industry, scrapers have come a long way since I began painting. The handles, grips, and blades have improved 100%. Stanley, Wooster, Sandvik, Wagner, and Red Devil are some of the better-crafted scrapers on the market. Scrapers like Sandvik that use carbide blades are worth considering because they resist nicks and dents from nails. The only drawback is that carbide blades can't be sharpened with a mil file. Other blades can, but they won't hold their edge as long, which is one reason box scrapers have multiple edges for fast replacement.

A scraper I use for removing paint, and a thousand other things, is a 5-in-1 scraper (also known as a 4-in-1 or 6-in-1). This looks like a narrow putty knife with a thick blade. It is great for getting at hard-to-reach spots, probing peeling or blistered paint, opening cans, lifting staples, and much more. I wrap a 5-in-1 with a rag to clean excess paint off trim work.

You should only scrape the surfaces where the paint is blistered, peeling, or cracked. Scrape with the grain, using measured, even strokes. Going against the grain will pit the wood. Bear in mind that all the scraped areas will have to be sanded and feathered out later for a smooth top coat (see p. 48), so make sure that you scrape only the places that need it. Paint and stain that appear to be in good shape should just be wire-brushed or sanded to prepare them as a base for the next coat.

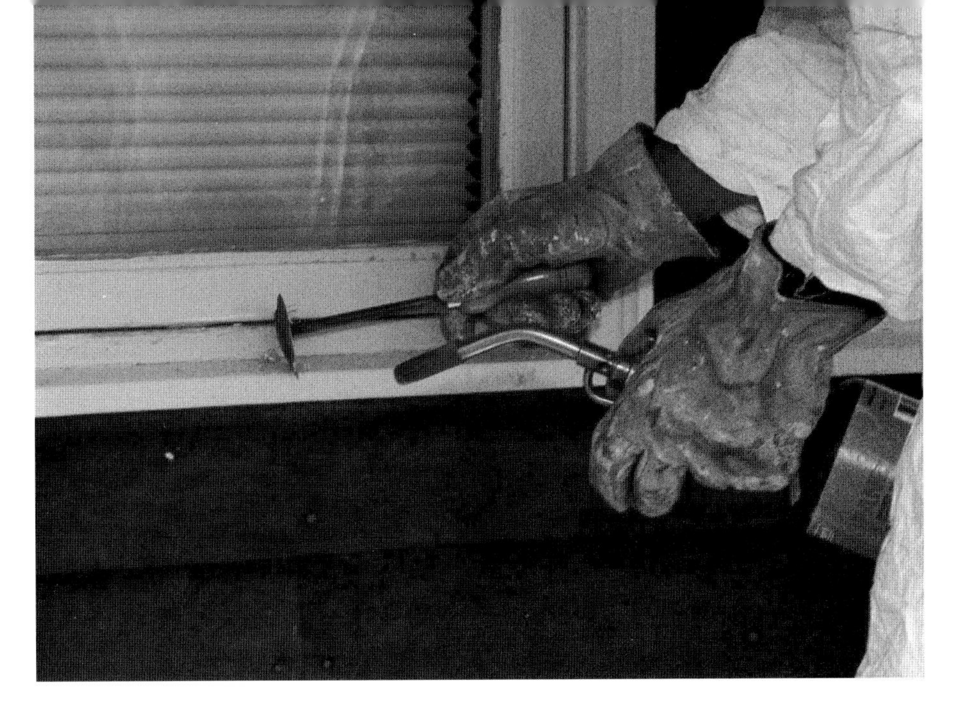

A triggered torch and a shave-hook do a great job of getting resistant flakes and cracked paint off siding. Make a few quick passes with the torch, then follow right behind with the shave-hook. Thick gloves, goggles, a fire extinguisher, and a respirator are necessities. Don't forget to use drop cloths any time you're scraping paint.

It's important not to scrape any more than you can sand and prime before the day is over. This is most important on exteriors during the wet months. If you leave a sanded area overnight, the paint will keep peeling and you'll have to resand everything the next day. I use a simple formula for prep work to make sure I don't get too far ahead of the priming coat: What takes three hours to scrape and sand will normally take one hour to prime. Just to be safe, limit your scraping to two hours at a time. That way, you should have enough time to finish sanding and priming before you have to quit for the day.

After using a box scraper, I go back over the surface with a shave-hook and torch to feather, or blend, the scraped areas. This is a practice I use almost exclusively on exteriors.

Before you begin with the shave-hook and torch, check to see what kind of insulation is under the siding. Once I started scraping and torching the siding of a house that was insulated with newspaper. Luckily I saw what was happening and put out the fire, but it could have been a real problem.

SANDERS AND SANDPAPER

Unfortunately, there are few if any painting projects that don't call for some sanding. You can minimize the tedium of sanding if you wear gloves and a respirator and if you have user-friendly tools (music usually helps, too). Remember: The finish coat will reflect all the effort you put into making the undercoats smooth. Even the best paint won't hide ragged edges left by scraping, or rough, uneven undercoats—but a good sanding will.

I stock an assortment of sandpapers for different coatings and finishes. If I'm using an electric sander, I avoid coarse grits, which can leave marks that are almost impossible to erase. I use 80 to 320 grit or higher for interior trim work with an orbital sander; I normally use 320 grit when I need a very fine paper, but you can go even higher than that. I use 36 to 220 grit for exterior work, depending on whether I'm doing rough or smooth sanding.

Be careful sanding windowsills and sashes—glass scratches very easily. Keep the sanding sponge or sandpaper about ½ in. away from the edge of the glass. At the end, carefully make one stroke with the sandpaper along the edge of the window.

Grinders are excellent for feathering wood porches and siding, reshaping split eaves, removing rust, and doctoring other exterior surfaces. Grinders tend to spew fine bits of stinging material, so wear a face shield and Tyvek suit.

Edge sanders take a lot of the work out of hand-sanding. They can get into grooves and corners that would otherwise eat up a great deal of time and elbow grease. I prefer the heavy-duty edge sander made by Fine.

Hand-sanding

Any place with an edge that has been stripped, scraped, or filled in will need to be feathered with sandpaper. The technique I use most often for interior trim is to use a very rough sandpaper, such as a floor-sanding grit, to begin feathering the edges. Then I graduate to the next finer grit, usually a medium grit, wrapped around a sanding sponge. I like to save the sanding sponge itself for the final sanding before priming. After priming, I sand between every coat with a lighter 220-grit to 320-grit sandpaper, using my finger to feel for surface irregularities.

Power-sanding

Sanding by hand is hard work. I use a grinder, belt sander, or random orbit sander whenever possible. Milwaukee and Porter-Cable make some of the best sanders (and other power tools). Other reputable brands include DeWalt and Black & Decker.

I use belt sanders for surfaces that have become uneven from paint build-up or warping, such as floors, decks, and porches. These are powerful tools that can leave ugly gouges, so apply a minimum of pressure at the start; as you get used to the sander, you can slowly add more pressure. When I'm using a belt sander, I cover up from head to foot and keep my knees well-padded.

Random orbit palm sanders are best for doors and trim work wide enough to accommodate a vibrating 4-in. square. Never use more than a medium grit on a palm sander or you'll be left with sanding swirls that are very hard to remove. Some palm sanders make your hands feel like jelly from poor shock absorption; use a quality sander.

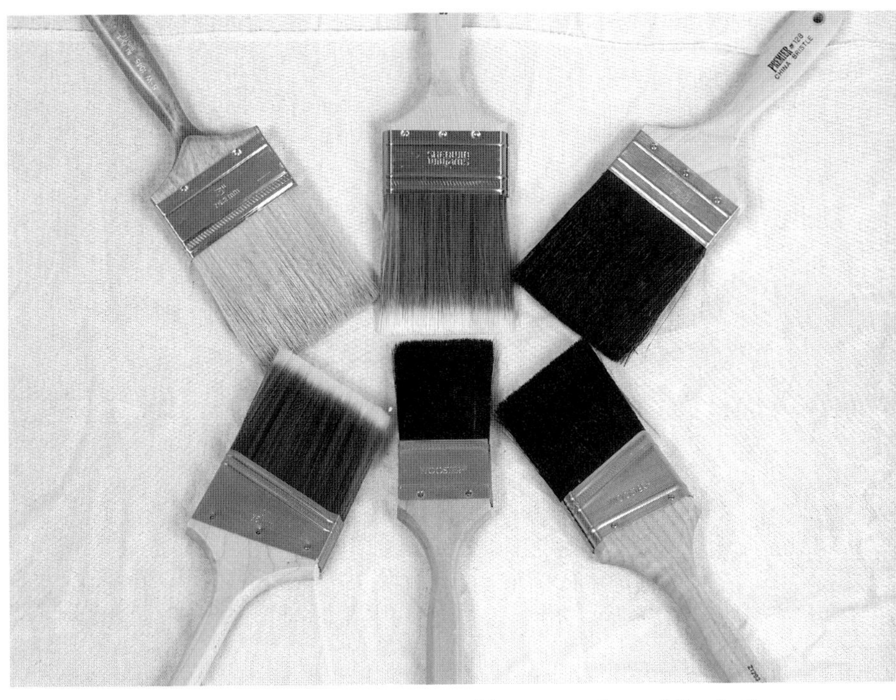

Here are a few of the better brands of brushes (Purdy, my favorite line, isn't shown). Clockwise from the top: Sher-Tip 3-in. trim brush with nylon/poly fill (latex); Premier 3-in. trim with black China bristle (oil); Wooster 2½-in. angled sash with fine China bristle (oil); Wooster 2-in. flat sash with China bristle (oil); Wooster 3-in. angled sash with nylon/poly (latex); Proval 3-in. enamel, varnish, and stain white China bristle.

BRUSHES

There are four styles of brushes: wall brushes, enamel and varnish brushes, flat sash brushes, and angled sash brushes. Wall brushes come in 3-in. and 4-in. widths, and are used mainly for interior walls and ceilings and for exterior surfaces such as siding. Enamel and varnish brushes range in widths from 1 in. to 3 in. These are used mostly for trim painting with oil-based paints or clear coatings. Enamel and varnish brushes have distinctive "beaver-tail" handles, thick fill, and tapered ends for precision painting. Flat sash brushes are the same width as enamel brushes, but have long, thin handles for hard-to-reach trim and windows. They are made for both latex and oil-based paints. Angled sash brushes have a diagonal edge for greater accuracy with angles and corners. Their narrow construction makes them the best for reaching tough spots like window corners. These brushes are also made in 1-in. to 3-in. widths.

Brush types are determined by the brush filaments, or "fill." China bristle, made from hogs, remains the favorite for all types of oil-based coatings. The roughness of a China bristle gives it more holding power, while the flattened end of the bristle deposits the paint smoothly. Black China bristle is a finer fill than white, which is used for trim and sash brushes. Only use China bristle brushes with oil-based coatings; they absorb water and lose their "snap" when they become saturated.

All better-quality synthetic brushes combine nylon and polyester. Nylon outlasts bristle, but pure nylon brushes are a bit springy and tend to spatter. Polyester is more chemical- and temperature-resistant than nylon and has about the same stiffness as natural bristle. Together, nylon and polyester make a fill that picks up ("loads") and spreads paint uniformly and evenly. Latex paint spreads best with synthetic fill; these brushes also work quite well with oil paints. However, it's a good idea to use each brush with only one type of paint. I label each brush cover "latex" or "oil."

Here are some special paint applicators. Clockwise from left: a paint mitt for radiators, fences, pipes, railings, and other unbrushable surfaces; a masonry brush that's good for undercoating masonry; a corner painting pad that attaches to an extension pole; a paint edger; an extension pole.

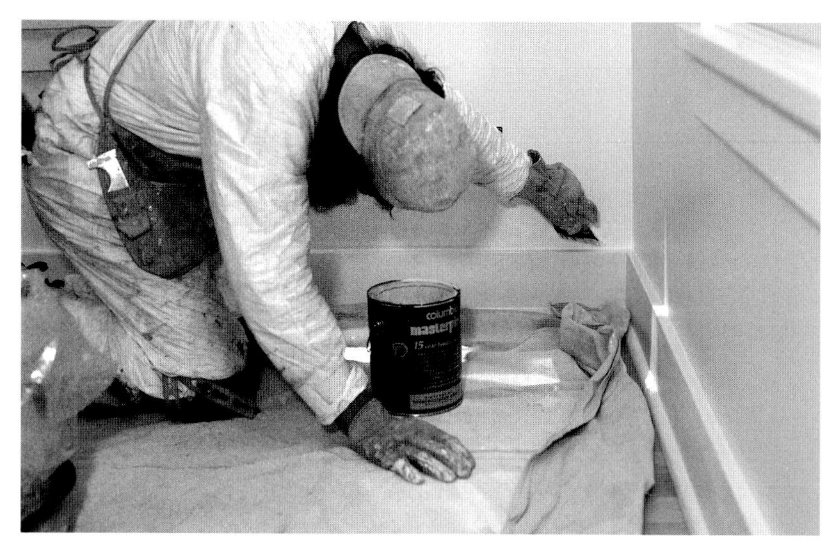

Switching hands rests your strong hand and increases your concentration. You'll find that you compensate for the loss of coordination in your weaker hand by using your entire arm. This helps you paint a straight line that might rival your strong hand's work.

Before buying a brush, remove the covering and check the condition of the bristles. (Better brushes are wrapped in protective cardboard.) The fill should be full-bodied and free of loose bristles. Check for a smooth, even taper at the end of the fill. Tapering adds strength to the fill, guarantees even coating, and extends the life of a brush. Flex the brush: A good brush has a moderate flex for smooth coating.

I let the type of job dictate the width and cut of the brush I'm using. In general, the more intricate the work, the narrower the brush. For most trim work, I use a 3-in. angled sash brush. For walls and ceilings, I use a 4-in. wall brush. For brushing on stains and clear coats, I use a 2-in. to 3-in. varnish brush.

Brushing techniques

Hold the brush toward the base, so your hand wraps around the handle. This gives you better control and makes pushing or pulling the brush a natural movement, turning the brush into an extension of your whole arm and keeping your wrist from getting overworked. Holding the brush farther up the handle tends to cause spatters. The only time I hold a brush by the end of the handle is when I'm reaching, but I'm always careful to make the stroke a pulling or pushing motion.

Painting with your opposite hand reduces the amount of reaching and twisting you have to do and also reduces ladder movement. By doubling your reach, you cut ladder movement in half.

The most effective brushing technique is to unload paint from the top down and from the middle out. Unload the brush in the middle of the stroke length (1 ft. to 2 ft.), and spread the paint evenly in both directions. Starting the brush stroke in the middle of the stroke length lets you control how much paint gets to the edge and corners.

If you're painting a corner while standing on a ladder, you'll find it far easier to switch hands than to twist around to reach the other side or to climb down and move the ladder. Less time spent climbing up and down means more time painting, and it's also easier on your knees.

Loading and unloading the brush
With your paint bucket filled about 3 in., load the brush and lightly slap it against the rim of the can to remove excess paint. Simply wiping the brush against the side of the can tends to clean off only one side of the brush, leaving the other overloaded and prone to dripping. I know a paint contractor who likes to "thunk" his brush straight down into the paint and wipe off both sides, so it's loaded in the middle and drip-free on the outside. Everyone has their own preferences for loading their brush—just avoid overloading it.

When you unload the paint, keep your brush moving at a steady pace, to avoid pooling. When a brush is placed on a surface, paint flows down the brush and onto the surface. Lift the brush and paint will stop flowing down the bristles, unless the brush has been overloaded.

Overloading damages your brush. Even after you think you've unloaded all the paint in your brush, there is still plenty left in the fill. Paint works its way to the base of the brush; when it dries, it spreads the bristles out and eventually turns the brush into a "club." After a brush "clubs," the shortened fill won't let the bristles hold much paint, and they have a tendency to streak. (Don't throw the brush out—you can still use it for priming or painting rough surfaces. The softer nylon/polyester brushes make good dusters.)

The finishing stroke A finishing stroke, also called a "feathering" stroke, minimizes brush marks. You need to feather trim, especially around windows and doors where smooth finishes are most noticeable. Feathering a stroke is a bit

Use a light touch for a finishing stroke. To feather brush marks, hold the brush at an angle and lift it at the end of each stroke.

like a plane landing and taking off again: It requires having your brush in motion before you contact the surface and removing the brush before you finish the stroke. Start a finishing stroke at the bottom and pull up. Toward the end of the stroke, slow the brush almost to a stop, turn it 45 degrees, lightly wiggle it, and then lightly pull it away. Master that and you'll have a smooth finish stroke with few brush marks. A top-quality paint with good flow and coverage also helps to hide brush marks. Always go back over a completed section and check for any drips or runs.

The ideal finishing stroke is one without any stops. If you're using good paint with the right additives (see p. 24), your brush will travel several feet in one stroke without pulling the paint. A 7-ft. stroke, most often used for vertical door trim, takes some practice, but it will save you time from having to feather smaller strokes. Window casings and sashes are usually of shorter length, which makes them a good place to learn to feather. A good finishing stroke takes practice, so I advise mastering it with trim that gets less attention.

Back-brushing is a type of feathering done over trim that has been rolled or sprayed. A roller cover leaves a stipple, and paint sprayed too thick on trim such as doors will leave an "orange peel" texture unless it's back-brushed. Limit your back-brushing to however much you can do before the paint begins to set up.

ROLLERS

To figure out which roller cover is best for your project, you need to consider the type of paint, the texture of the surface, and the smoothness of the finish that you want. There's a roller cover for every type of paint and surface, but I tend to stick with a super-thick nap such as lambswool, which holds quite a bit of paint. Although lambswool isn't recommended for latex—alkali in the paint will eventually rot the leather—I've never had a problem. Pittsburgh Paints makes a lambswool cover called "Shearling" that can be used for both oil and latex paints. It has a synthetic core that won't rot with repeated exposure to water.

Mohair is a natural fabric with a much shorter nap than lambswool (3⁄16 in.). Mohair is a "Cadillac" fiber that leaves a super-smooth texture and is ideal for applying glossy oil paints and varnishes without any stipple. (A glossy coating with a stippled finish gives the surface a rough, textured look.)

Synthetic fabrics work well with most paints, especially flat latexes. They come in several thicknesses, with longer naps designed for rolling paint on rough surfaces. A nap of 1 in. to 1¼ in. is recommended for rougher textures such as brick and stucco. Remember that the longer the nap, the more paint the cover will hold—that's my top priority. I always use a high-quality roller with a nap that is 25% longer than recommended. This lets me spend time spreading paint instead of making trips back and forth to the rolling pan.

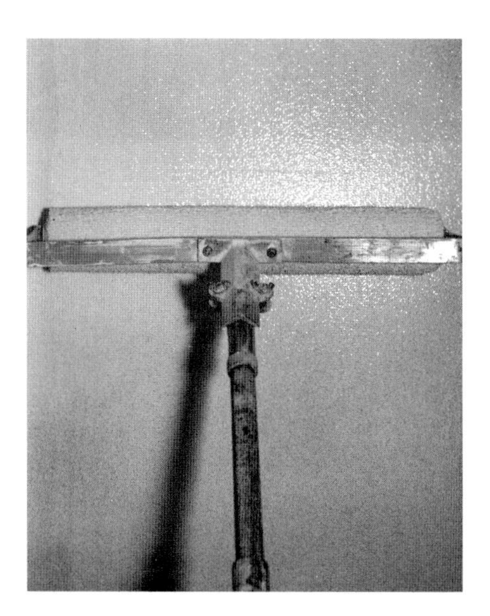

Most walls and ceilings need some stipple for added depth and dimension. The rougher the roller cover's nap, the more stipple it will leave. Stipple direction is determined by the finishing stroke of the roller, so keep your final strokes going in the same direction.

Better roller covers have beveled edges that let you paint close to edges and corners without leaving a thick seam. The closer you can paint to an edge, the less cutting in you have to do. Cutting in provides a neat edge around trim, corners, and angles that are hard to reach with a roller. The usual method for cutting in is to brush a 3-in. band of paint that later will be overlapped by a roller. Thick new paints and better roller covers have greatly reduced the amount of cutting in you have to do: I can roll within an inch or two of an edge or corner. One contractor I know rolls first, then goes back and cuts in. Rolling close to the edge takes practice and skill, but it saves time if you do it cleanly—you only need to cut in as far as the rolled paint.

The roller cover should be dampened before you use it, to prime and "de-fuzz" it. If you're rolling latex, wet the cover with water; if you're rolling an oil-based paint, use thinner. Spin out the excess water or thinner with a brush/roller spinner, or squeeze it out manually and towel the roller with a lint-free rag. Roller covers can also be de-fuzzed by wrapping masking tape around your hand and using your hand as a lint brush.

You may want to use a 5-gallon bucket with a roller grid instead of a roller pan. The grid hangs from the top of the bucket and allows for quicker paint loading, without the spattering you often experience with a roller pan. With a grid you load down instead of out. Roller pans have a habit of tipping easily—you think you know exactly where the pan is while you're rolling a ceiling, and before you know it you have your foot in it. You might bump into a 5-gallon bucket, but you probably will

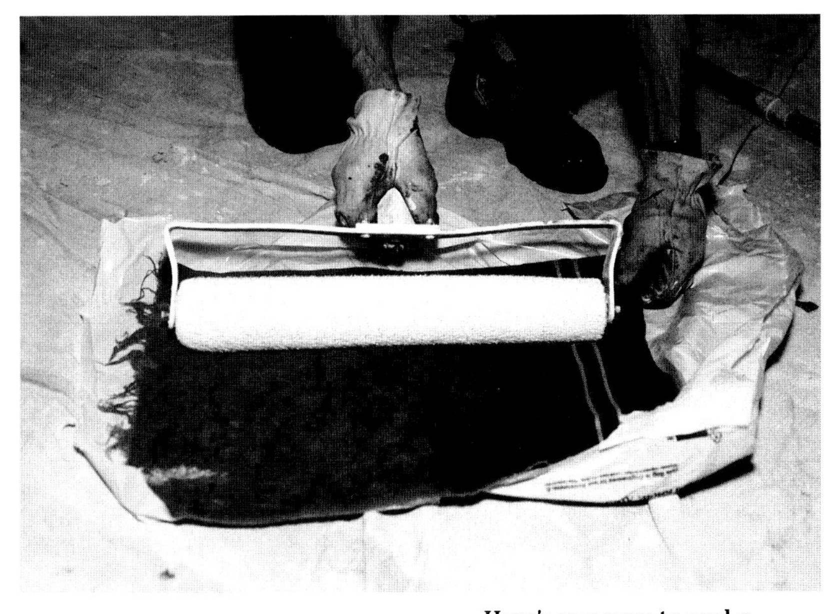

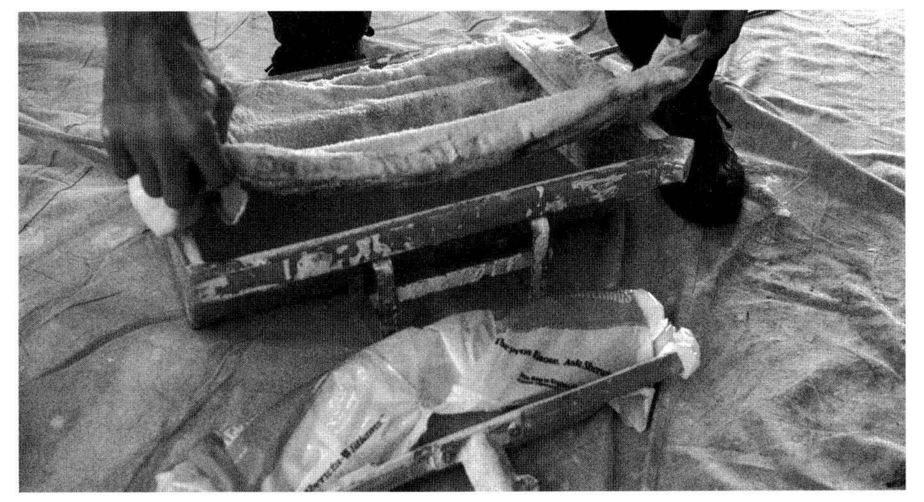

Here's one way to seal a roller cover and roller pan. I wrap the cover in a damp towel and seal it with a large piece of plastic (top). To keep paint from drying in the pan, I simply place another damp towel over the pan (left). Note the width of the roller cover—18 in., double the standard width. These long rollers require a special pan.

You won't always need to stretch this far, but extension poles are important tools. They save you from climbing ladders, and they speed up the job.

never step in one. It also takes longer to get the roller evenly coated using a pan (though filling the pan only half-full helps).

A good fiberglass or aluminum roller extension is one painting tool worth having. It will save your back and add to the length of your stroke, for better coverage. Just be careful not to spread the paint too thin. Resist the temptation to buy an inexpensive wooden extension. The soft wood will keep giving out and you'll spend more time tightening the sections than you will rolling. A good fiberglass extension stays put when you lock it.

Electric home power rollers have a self-contained supply of paint, which saves trips back and forth to the roller pan. However, power rollers require that you carry the paint supply on your back. This can be cumbersome, and you still have to stop to refill the tank. Cleaning the whole thing takes longer than cleaning a roller cover (see Chapter 6). Power rollers also are a little noisy. For me, these fall into the "not-altogether-necessary gizmo" category, but you be the judge.

Roller techniques

Rolling is one of the best ways to spread and finish an even coat of paint. A roller has the same function as a brush: It unloads, spreads, and blends paint with finishing strokes. The traditional method of unloading paint has been to roll it out in a zigzag like an "N" or a "Z." That method is still good for rougher surfaces; the paint should be spread in all directions for better coverage. However, newer, thicker paints also can be rolled in vertical lines with a 2-in. overlap to blend the paint. Rolling in straight lines keeps the paint from getting spread too thin. A thick roller cover assures you of a thicker coat, no matter how you choose to unload the paint.

After unloading and spreading a roller full of paint, go back over the area with lighter blending strokes. When blending, be careful to stroke in one direction for a uniform stipple.

The key to getting a good coat with a roller is to apply the paint thickly and evenly, but not to overload it. Keep in mind that better paints, especially latex paints, can be applied more thickly than you might think. Too often a rolled coat is spread way too thin, which makes even the best paint look bad and come off with the first washing.

SPRAYERS

You don't need much training to operate an airless sprayer. Basic sprayers take 10 minutes to learn how to use, and most professional paint shops will gladly show you. Technique and safety are crucial for a professionally sprayed job, so take your time learning how to do it right. Once you get going with a sprayer you'll be amazed at how fast you can coat the whole job. Sprayers can apply a very thick coat, much thicker than a brush.

Most homeowners rent paint sprayers because of their cost. I recommend renting from a paint store, which is more likely to have the equipment you need and the expertise to get you going. Paint stores are also more likely to have both airless and high-volume, low pressure (HVLP) professional sprayers. Whether you rent or buy a sprayer, I strongly advise getting a checklist for the operation and cleaning.

Airless sprayers

These are the most common type of sprayers—and the most powerful. They're connected to a compressor that's used to pump up to 3,000 psi (pounds per square inch) of paint through a hose. Pressure is regulated on the compressor pump, and the spray gun is fitted with a tip that determines how wide the spray fan will be. If you rent an airless sprayer, the gun you use probably will have a 10-in. fan.

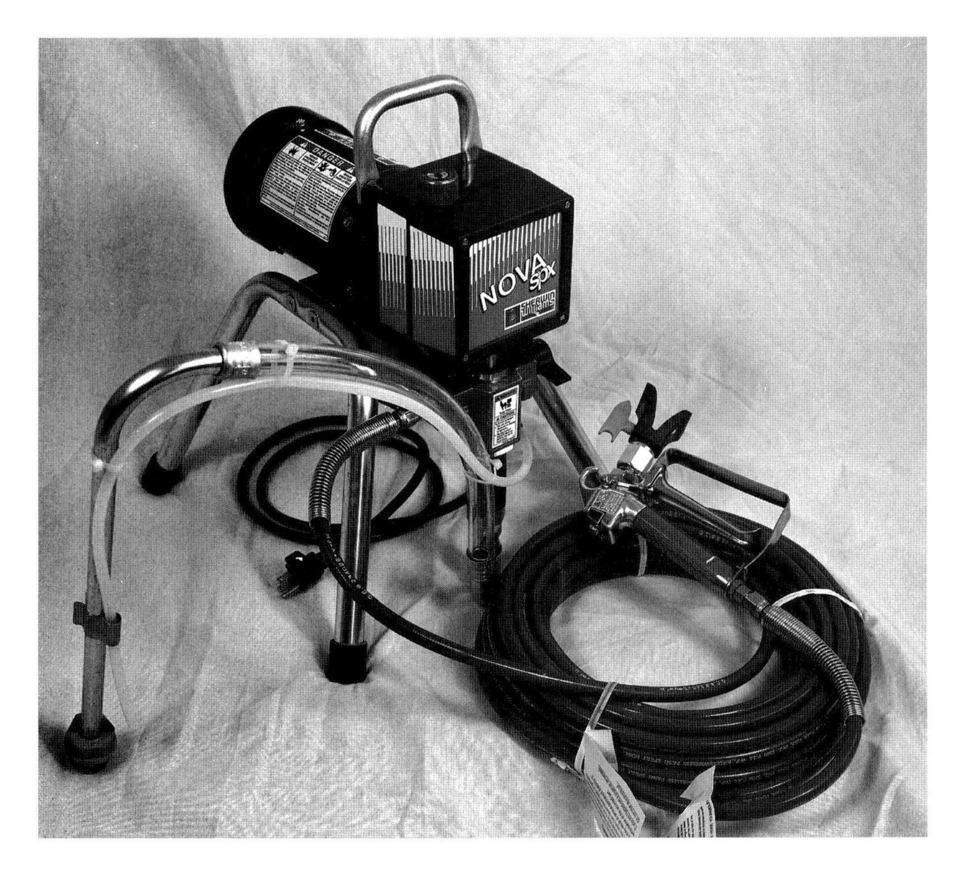

The Sherwin Williams Nova spx is a portable, compact airless sprayer that weighs only 34 pounds. This model can be rented with a 25-ft. hose and spray gun.

A spray shield can be easily made from anything that is light and rigid, such as cardboard or paneling. You'll need one straightedge for the shield to work. I usually make a 2-ft. by 5-ft. shield, which is easy to handle. Spray shields get thick with paint after a while, so it's best to have several on hand for big jobs.

Sprayer extensions make spraying easy. The added distance is another benefit: You can see your work better without getting a face full of spray.

Airless sprayers have a feed tube with a screened end that is placed inside the paint source, usually a 5-gallon bucket filled with 2 or 3 gallons. The line has to be uncoiled and straightened out before you can start spraying. To prime the line, you simply turn on the pump, which pumps for about 10 seconds and stops when the line is full. Then the airless is ready to go.

Most spraying accessories are designed for professional work, but they can really speed up a paint job. The Scroller is an attachment for airless sprayers that reduces overspray and back-rolls the paint at the same time, for better penetration and even coverage. Accessories for the home user include spray shields, spray extensions, and goggles with changeable lenses.

Airless sprayers create quite a bit of overspray. Spray shields act as moveable masking. They keep overspray to a minimum but don't eliminate it entirely. I use them mostly for protecting walls, ceilings, and rooftops when a clean line isn't needed. For instance, I may use a shield on areas that have been primed, such as baseboard trim, when I'm spraying a latex on the walls and want keep it off the trim.

Sprayer extensions are spray guns with a 3-ft. nozzle. Like extension poles for rollers, they let you cover a lot of ground with much less reaching. Extensions also allow you to get a straight, even stroke instead of circular arcs. They aren't always available in rental packages, but get one if you can; you'll save yourself time and strain.

Techniques If you've never used an airless sprayer before, you should practice on a large piece of paneling or cardboard until you feel comfortable (see the photo below). Most paint gun triggers are designed to be used with the first two fingers. The remaining fingers hold the base of the gun for control. When you first pull the trigger on an airless, you'll notice how fast the paint comes out. First try a dry run with the trigger deactivated.

Before I begin spraying, I uncoil and lay out the hose, setting the spray gun at the point I want to paint first. I clear the area of unnecessary items that might snag the hose; I don't want to have to stop in midstroke to free my equipment.

Sprayed paint "loads up" quickly, and it runs faster than brushed or rolled paint. As a result, spraying demands precise, quick strokes—about 3 ft. per second. Hold the gun approximately 10 in. from the surface and begin moving it before you start spraying. Use your other hand

Before you start spraying, try a test shot on a large piece of cardboard or paneling. At first you might see a little spitting at the end of a stroke. This probably will go away as the pressure equalizes in the line. If your gun gets clogged, loosen the tip and turn it 180 degrees, then tighten it and trigger the gun to blow out the clog.

For large areas such as siding, doors, walls, and ceilings, run the sprayer as long as you can to keep your momentum going. Use a quick, whip-like motion on the return sweep; it will keep paint from getting too thick at the end of the stroke.

to keep the hose clear and to keep pressure off the hose-gun connection. Keep the gun as parallel to the surface as you can, using a back-and-forth sweeping motion. Avoid a circular motion or you'll end up with an uneven coat. I'm careful to overlap half the fan width with each spray stroke. This helps to ensure an even coat.

Check your work frequently for runs and missed areas. Pay special attention to the tops of doors and the tops and bottoms of your spray strokes. Pause to check every 5 to 10 minutes, before the paint begins drying. Have a brush or roller handy to feather any touch-ups you need to make.

Corners require special attention when you're spraying. The majority of corners you'll encounter with interior work are "inside" corners that angle away from you. "Outside" corners are more common on exteriors. The technique for both is the same: A vertical motion with the gun held at 90 degrees. Avoid overlapping the corner to keep paint from building up. Outside corners require a quick stroke to prevent paint from loading up on the edge.

Safety When paint comes out of an airless sprayer, the pressure is enough to tear through skin. A small flange protrudes about 1½ in. from the tip of the spray gun to keep the nozzle away from skin. However, the flange isn't foolproof. Use caution whenever you spray with an airless, especially when you're moving on a ladder or scaffolding. Should an accident occur, get medical attention quickly. Latex paint is more dangerous than oil paint if it's injected under the skin; the chemicals mix faster with blood. Dressing right, which includes gloves, greatly reduces the risks involved with spraying. Avoid spraying when you're tired. I always try to spray early in the day, when I'm at my sharpest.

HVLP sprayers are excellent for spraying trim because reduced overspray and improved control mean less masking. This HVLP sprayer's paint supply is held in a pint container attached to the gun.

HVLP sprayers

A newer type of sprayer is the High Volume/Low Pressure sprayer, or HVLP. These sprayers are easy to operate; you really only have to point and spray. HVLPs spray much more slowly than airless sprayers. The lower pressure is great for control, minimizing wasteful overspray and requiring comparatively little masking. HVLPs also are much safer to use; you only need to protect your eyes. But because the pressure is so low, HVLPs aren't recommended for painting large areas. They're best for finish work such as closets, furniture, louvered doors, pipes, cabinets—any surface where control is needed. The HVLP technique also is different: You stop the gun at the end of each stroke.

PAINTING ACCESSORIES

A few simple tools will make your painting project easier, longer-lasting, and a lot more comfortable to work on.

Caulk and caulk guns

Since you're saving money by doing the job yourself, spend a few extra dollars on long-lasting caulk and a top-quality caulk gun. They'll help give you professional results. Inexpensive caulks won't hold up well, and cheaper caulk guns don't last long.

First, get the tube of caulk ready. It's important to cut the tip at the proper angle to get a good bead. Cut the tip close to the end of the tube at a 45-degree angle. If in doubt where to make

This dripless caulk gun eliminates wasted caulk and time-consuming clean-up. I always go for a smaller bead of caulk on interior work and use my little finger to press it. Outside, I use my index finger.

the opening, cut closer to the edge—if it's too small, you can always enlarge it. If you don't get a perfect cut, or if you end up with too big an opening, mask the area you're working on to keep excess caulk from getting everywhere. Masking is always a good idea for silicone caulk, which is very slippery and has a tendency to spread.

After you've cut the tip, break the seal with the seal break that swings out from the bottom of the caulk frame. If your gun doesn't have a seal break, use a hanger wire. Don't use framing nails—they're too thick. I usually break the seal with a length of 10- or 12-gauge wire; anything larger makes the caulk come out too fast.

The "less is better" idea definitely applies to caulk. Spread the caulk at a slow and steady rate, leaving a narrow bead. Then make one or two passes over the bead with a dampened finger to press the caulk in place and remove any excess. The right size bead will leave little excess to clean up. Have wet and dry rags nearby to keep your hands and surfaces clean. I keep a 1- or 5-gallon bucket one-third full of warm water close by, for rinsing the caulk rag. Hint: If you have lots of caulking to do, I recommend taping a rubber glove finger over your caulking finger to prevent a blister.

Wire brushes

Wire brushes combine the abrasiveness of sandpaper and the cleaning power of a brush. I mainly use wire brushes for cleaning paint brushes and for loosening dirt and rust. The old style of wire brush had a straight handle that got the job done, but often skinned my knuckles in the process. Now there's a new generation of brushes, such as those made by Wooster, that have wrap-around, knuckle-saving handles as well as a better angle for improved leverage.

Braces and pads

Like many people in an active line of work, I never thought I'd have back problems. But after years of unsupported lifting, I've joined the ranks of those who have pushed their lower back one lift too far. I don't think twice anymore about wearing a back brace. Braces really do help distribute the weight around your torso, protecting you from the strain of brushing, rolling, crouching, climbing ladders, bending, and lifting. They can be easily purchased at home centers, hardware stores, and athletic supply stores.

You will most likely be painting from the ceiling to the floor and spending a lot of time on your knees. There are two types of knee pads: heavy-duty rubber pads

Once you've accidentally knelt on something sharp, you'll understand the value of knee pads.

and the lighter foam athletic knee pads. I use the heavy pads for working on the floor—when I'm prepping trim, masking, or cutting in the baseboard (see the photo above). The lighter pads are handy for bracing my knees against ladders.

If the joints in your stronger arm tend to act up, you also should consider wearing a wrist or elbow brace. Many painting tasks involve repetitive motion. Even a perfectly healthy wrist can become inflamed. Joint braces can be found at most drug stores.

Swivel hooks

Swivel hooks are a helpful ladder accessory—and at least $3 apiece, an excellent investment (see the photo at right). They keep a paint bucket level and accessible and help prevent spills. You can buy them at paint stores and some hardware stores.

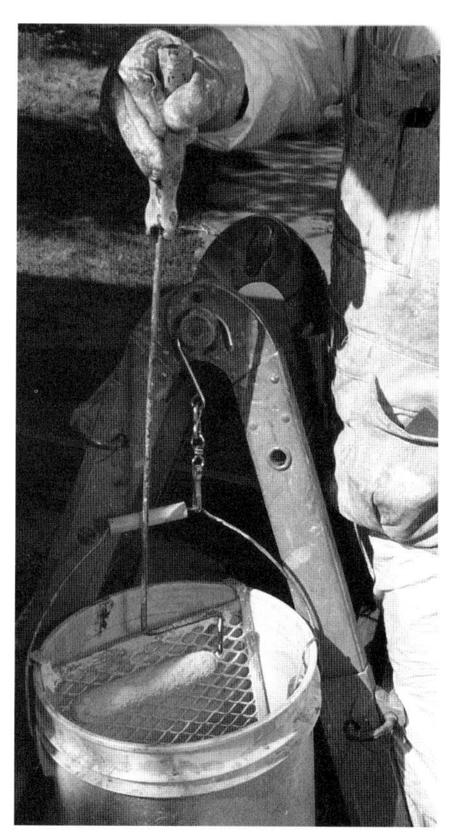

Swivel hooks are a great item for securing a paint bucket to a ladder. They give the bucket flexible movement—important when you're working off a ladder. With fixed hooks you have to use both hands to load the brush.

Posture and Stretching

Stretching tones the muscles and readies them for activity, and it is also an effective stress reliever. I avoid heavy stretching before work in the morning; I'm not warmed up and the chances of pulling a muscle are greater. I tend to do more stretching as the day progresses—say, when my wrist or arm starts feeling fatigued. It also feels good to take a minute or two to stretch my back or legs. I do more serious stretching at the end of the day. Everything's warm and limbered up by then, and a good stretch keeps overworked joints and muscles, especially in my back, loosened up for the next day.

You've probably compared the gas mileage your car gets in town with its highway mileage. The same concept of energy efficiency applies to all types of motion, including painting.

Being in a hurry inevitably leads to stops and starts, mistakes and aggravation. Thoughtful motion, on the other hand, helps with concentration and actually speeds up the entire project. If you've ever watched professionals in the building trades, you may have noticed that they keep a steady pace and motion. They pay attention to what they're doing, and know exactly where they are in the process.

When you're mindful of your movements, you'll find that it's easier to concentrate on things like getting a smoother painting stroke. If you're brushing, focus on bringing your entire arm into the picture. The same goes for scraping, where you can use more of your torso to get a better stroke. Smoother movement comes down to being more aware of what you're doing and how you're doing it, and seeing if there's a better way.

Stretching only takes a few minutes and delivers big returns. To stretch the backs of your legs, form a "V" and alternate pushing your heels down. This stretch is also good for the back, shoulders, arms, and hands.

Next, bring one leg forward and carefully place your weight in back of the knee.

After loosening up both legs, drop your hips and lower back, placing your weight on the arms and shoulders. Any time you feel "tedium overload," take a break to loosen up stiff muscles and joints. You'll find yourself taking fewer pain pills.

4

PAINTING INTERIORS

Before you start painting, invest some time in planning the project and organizing your equipment. This will save you headaches and actually speed up the job, since you won't be wasting time cleaning up smudges and drips that could have been avoided, racing to the paint store for forgotten tools, or searching for tools you've misplaced. Having what you need will keep your momentum going. Also, a solid plan cuts any job down to size. You won't feel as if you've embarked on a bottomless project.

SETTING UP THE WORK AREA

The first thing you'll need to do is prepare the space you'll be working in. Good organization now will pay off in greater efficiency later.

You'll probably have to start by moving furniture. Furniture can be moved to the middle of the room, giving you a perimeter to work in, or to one side of the room, allowing you to paint in sections. I prefer to move as much of the furniture out of the room as possible. A small table is handy for laying out tools, but you'd be surprised how easy it is to trip over just one piece of furniture when you're moving around a room.

Next, plan your work layout. Ideally, you'll have two layout areas: a central location with tools and materials for the entire project, and another spot for the material needed in each room (see the top photo on the facing page). A basement or garage works best for the tool and material depot, but any room will work. Mentally divide the project into stages. Each room should contain only the equipment and materials necessary for a particular stage of the project—for example, prepping trim or sanding. Organizing a project this way will make

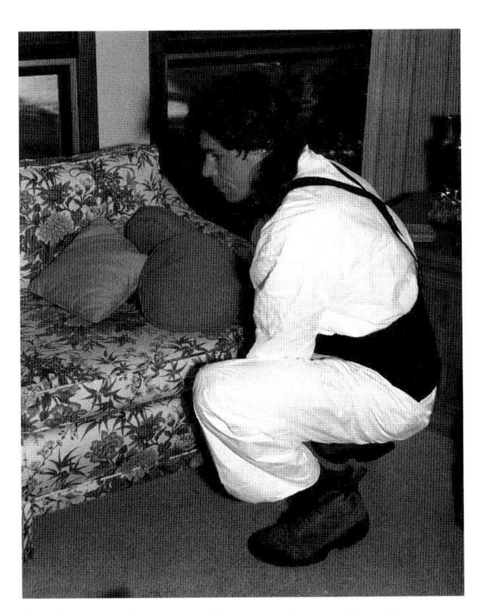

A cleared room is much easier to paint. Always wear a back support when lifting, even for small jobs.

This makeshift workbench, located in a garage, will serve as a supply area for all phases of the painting project.

it more manageable; fewer obstructions in a room will help the job flow smoothly. Don't set out your tools until the work area has been masked off and protected with drop cloths (see p. 38).

WALL AND CEILING PREPARATION

To start most projects, you'll need masking materials; pliers; a screwdriver or powerdriver for removing fixtures, doors, and hardware; and a container for the hardware you take off. Have masking tape, spackling, putty knife, and a caulking gun on hand for filling holes and hairline cracks in the ceiling and walls. You can keep these tools handy in a painting apron (shown in the photo at right).

Removing fixtures, hardware, and doors

The first step in prepping walls and ceilings is to remove all the fixtures, along with electrical outlet covers, nails, and

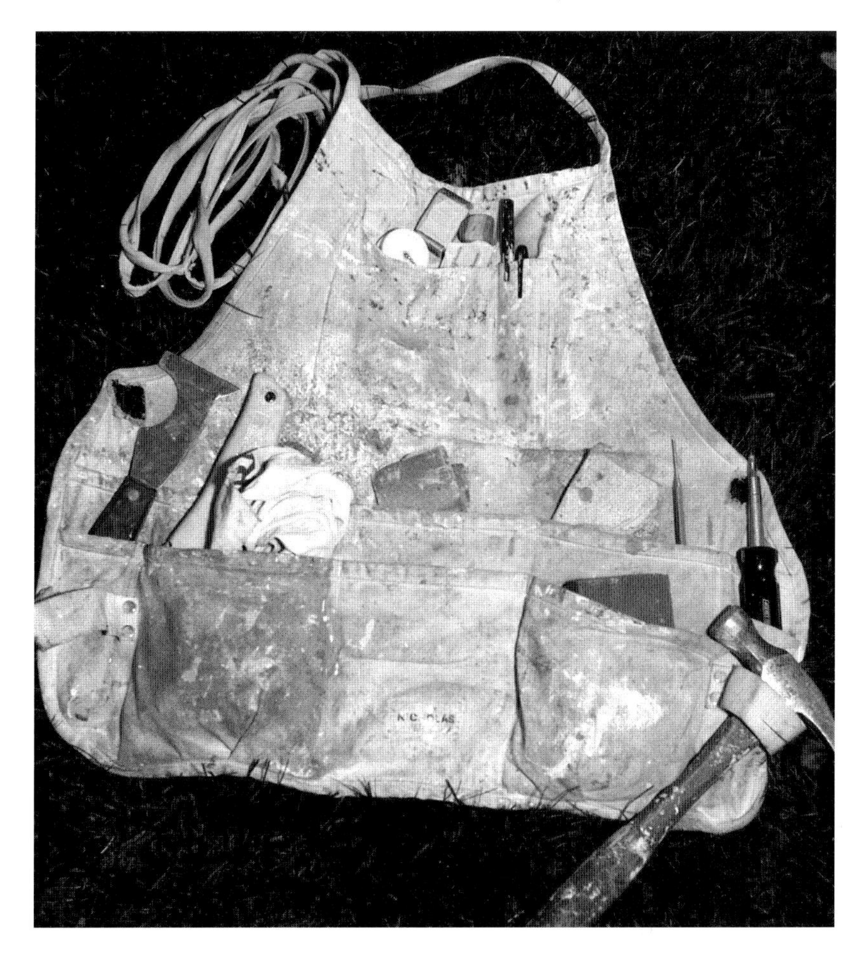

Painting aprons reduce trips to the tool layout area. Shown here: a 5-in-1 scraper, a dusting brush, a retractable razor and blades, Band-Aids, ear plugs, pens, a center punch, a 4-in-1 screwdriver, a wonder bar, sandpaper, a sanding sponge, a rag, and a utility knife.

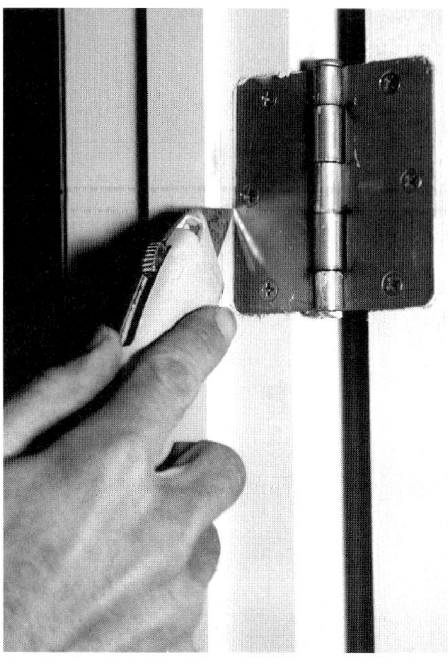

Hinge plates often need to be scored before you can remove them. If the knife score is sufficient, a 5-in-1 will take out the plate without ripping the paint.

plant and picture hangers. Bathrooms and kitchens take longer than other rooms because they have the lion's share of handles, racks and lights. Overhead light fixtures also need to be stripped down to the base, leaving just the cover to be masked. Hanging lights in the dining room and kitchen can be masked off if you plan to roll the area, but if you're going to spray you should disconnect and remove the fixtures.

For ease of access to the doors and door trim, I recommend taking the doors off their hinges and setting them aside. Remove the doors even if you don't plan to paint or refinish them—otherwise, you'll have to work around them. It only takes a few minutes to remove a door. There may be times when you want to leave the doors on, such as when you plan to paint the hardware (something I don't recommend). In these cases,

Labeling doors and cabinets

It's important to label all doors; they are not interchangeable. Write the door's location on masking tape at the top or inside a hinge. Then tape over that marking and label the door a second time. This precaution is especially important if you intend to spray the doors. The first label probably will be sprayed over and impossible to read.

Because cabinet doors are numerous, they require a schematic for keeping them straight. This means actually drawing a layout of the cabinets, using directions to number each one (for example, North3). Cabinets sometimes can be left on their hinges if they only need a new coat of paint and you intend to paint over the hardware.

The taping system used for standard doors won't work with cabinet doors because the entire cabinet door gets painted. As you remove each cabinet door, mark the least visible edge, top or bottom, with an engraver. Engraving is the best method of keeping track of the door's location—you can still read it after multiple coats of paint.

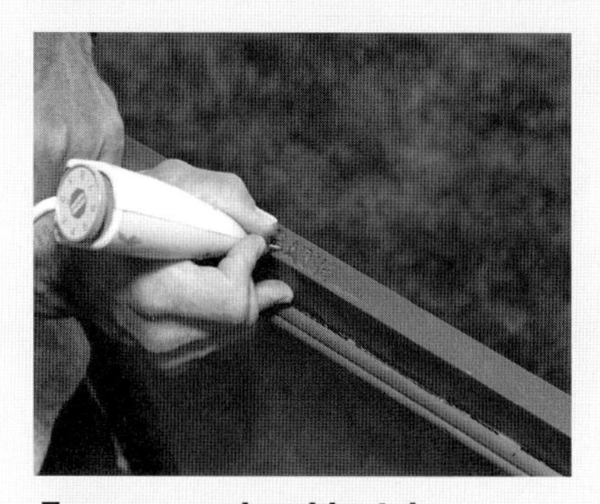

Engrave each cabinet door as soon as you've removed it. Engravers also work well for labeling screens and screen doors.

Paint will slough off after soaking for a few minutes in strong paint stripper. Be sure to have plenty of ventilation.

wedge the door open while you're prepping and painting it, but be careful not to put much pressure on the hinges.

It's a good idea to label everything you remove. It's the first thing I do after removing a door or piece of hardware. Unless you've labeled it, the hardware from even one room will provide you with plenty of time-consuming guesswork when you have to put it back.

Have a roll of masking tape on hand to label each set of hinges and hinge plates as soon as they come off. If the doors will be refinished, remove all hardware: hinges, hinge plates, and door knobs. Older knobs should just be masked off since they can be difficult to remove.

Stripping hardware

Stripping hardware such as hinges and hinge plates is easy if you use the right stripper, but exercise caution. The active ingredients in paint strippers are methyl chloride, which is caustic, and toluene, which gives off noxious vapors. Strippers such as Bix, however, are water soluble and "gray water safe" (environmentally acceptable). Be sure to use industrial-strength rubber gloves, a respirator, and good ventilation. Read the entire can twice to make sure you understand any warnings.

Soak the hardware in stripper for a few minutes. If the hardware has soaked long enough, the layers of paint should almost fall off, but you'll still need at least a toothbrush to get down to metal, and possibly a wire brush and scraper. After you remove most of the dissolved paint, soak the hardware in a bucket of warm water for about five minutes. Remove any remaining paint particles with synthetic steel wool or a 3M green scouring pad.

Treat one set of hardware at a time so you can relabel it after stripping it.

Removing wallpaper

It's usually best to remove wallpaper instead of painting over it. If the wall covering is in poor shape—if the seams are curling up or there are visible

You can't hurry wallpaper removal. This paper didn't want to come off; I had to double-steam it.

flaws—you should definitely remove it before you refinish the wall. Wet paint might make the paper bubble up or make the seams curl even worse.

I avoid painting over wallpaper that is highly textured or coming loose. On the occasions when I have painted over paper, I've gotten good results using latex primer. Before painting, I reglue any seams that need fixing, then wash the wallpaper.

Most wallpaper in bathrooms and kitchens is vinyl and peels off easily. Then all you need to do is wipe the wall with a sponge to clean off any remaining adhesive, and lightly sand it to give it some tooth. However, wallpaper in the rest of the house is probably glued on, so you'll have to steam it off or use wallpaper remover. No matter how easily the wallpaper comes off, the stripped paper will make a mess, so make sure drop cloths are in place before you start.

There are two methods of taking off wallpaper: electric steaming and liquid wallpaper remover. I prefer the steamer because it's easy and fast once you get the knack of using it. Wallpaper remover, on the other hand, requires quite a bit of paper scoring in order for the remover to penetrate and loosen the glue. This leaves small holes in the drywall or plaster that have to be filled later. One advantage of wallpaper remover is that it removes most of the wallpaper glue. However, I've found that steaming is quicker, even after sponging the walls to remove any remaining glue.

Don't worry about the occasional scratch left by a putty knife. I have yet to see a wall that didn't need touching up after wallpaper removal. A few more nicks won't make much difference. A well-maintained putty knife will reduce scratches. Knives that are nicked, rusted, or coated with dried compound create more problems than they fix.

Whether you use a steamer or liquid remover, the walls should be sanded with 180-grit paper to knock off any remaining wallpaper glue. A light sanding also evens out the surface and gets the walls ready to be primed.

Spackling

At first glance your walls and ceilings may appear to need little preparation. On closer inspection, however, you'll probably see dents and nail holes. Smaller holes can be repaired with spackle. Cracks and repairs larger than ½ in. should be skim-coated with drywall compound (see p. 70).

Spackling is simple to use, needs little preparation, and sands easily. Your finger is the best applicator, followed by a single pass with a putty knife (see the bottom photo at right). Use a moderate amount of pressure when applying spackle, to reduce the chance of shrinkage. Spackle dries out quickly, so keep the lid on the container.

In the course of spackling wall repairs, you might notice a raised ring around nail holes where the drywall skin has puckered up. These rings will leave a bump if you just spackle over them. I deal with these bumps by pressing the handle of a 5-in-1 scraper or putty knife over the hole to form a slight depression. For holes, I roll up a small piece of masking tape, plug the hole with it, then spackle and sand over it (see the top photo at right).

To sand spackle, you only need a fine grit of sandpaper and a light touch. Be careful or you will erase the spackle in no time. Lightly sand in two different directions to eliminate sanding marks.

Roll up a short piece of masking tape to make a hole plug. Stuff the plug into the hole and fill the rest with spackle.

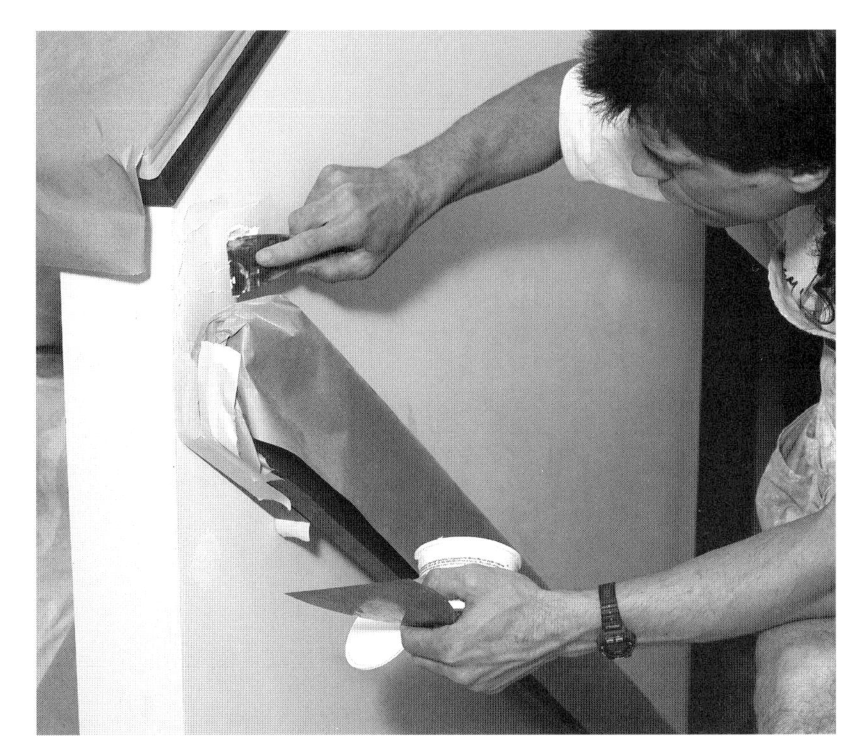

New spackles dry faster and shrink less. Here I'm skim-coating a thin layer of spackle over fingernail scratches. The spackle dried within 10 minutes, compared to hours for joint compound. After a quick sanding, it was ready to be painted.

Working with joint compound

Joint compound (or "mud," as it's known in the taping business) is the best material for substantial repairs such as cracks and sizable holes. Like spackle, mud goes on in layers and will shrink and crack if applied too thickly. It also sets up fast, allowing you only a few application strokes. Work it too much and you might tear it.

It takes practice to become good at taping and skim-coating. To see how it's really done, try watching tapers at work. Tapers clean their knives with every pass. They move fast, leaving just the right amount of mud over the tape and seam. A good taper leaves little to sand and a seamless joint after it's been painted.

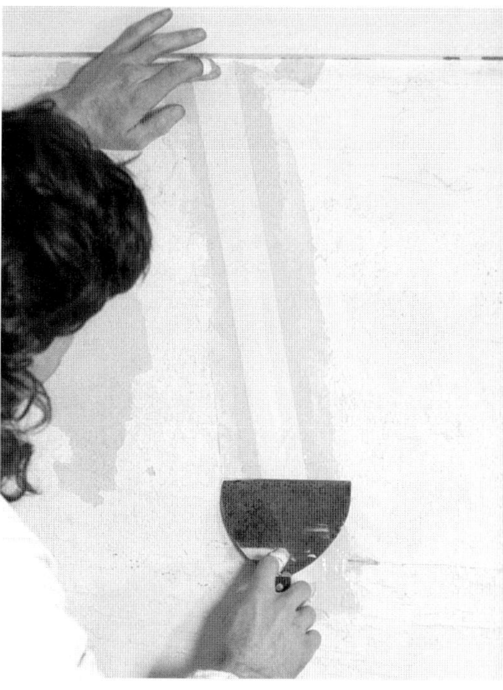

To repair cracks, measure the amount of tape you'll need (1) and cut it off with a broad knife. Apply a thin adhesive layer of mud over the crack (2) and place the tape over the area. On the next pass, cover the tape with mud (3). Clean your knife between passes—anything on the blade will leave a trail. Make only a few passes with the knife to smooth the mud, being careful not to tear the tape. Most repairs made with joint compound require at least two coats of mud, so don't try to hide the tape completely with the first coat.

PATCHING HOLES IN DRYWALL

Patching small holes in drywall (6 in. or less) is fast and easy, and you don't need to use drywall tape.

Before making a masking tape template, take a minute to clean out the hole—the squarer the hole, the easier it will be to cut the template. Cover the hole with strips of masking tape, then cut the tape around the edge of the hole (1). This gives you the template for a patch. Place the tape template on the back (rough) side of a piece of drywall that's at least 1½ in. larger than the outline of the template. Holes larger than 3 in. need greater support; make the patch 2 in. bigger all the way around.

Score around the template, but don't cut all the way through the drywall; you'll need to keep the skin intact to hold the patch over the hole. I cut the patch just a little smaller than the hole, to ensure a fit.

Carefully peel the drywall off the outside of the pattern (2). Set the patch in the hole to check the fit (you may need to size it slightly with a utility knife). Remove the patch and mud over the skin; this will hold the patch in place (3). Once the patch is set in the hole, skim a layer of mud on the exposed drywall paper to provide extra bonding (4).

Larger repairs call for a type of mud along the line of a dry putty, such as Mend-All, Bondo, or the Minwax two-part system. If you want the mud to set up quickly, try using a "hot" mud that hardens in 5 to 10 minutes. Surf-All and Rock-Hard are good hot muds. Only mix enough for one application. Hot muds are very hard to sand, but they can be smoothed with a wet rag before they set up completely.

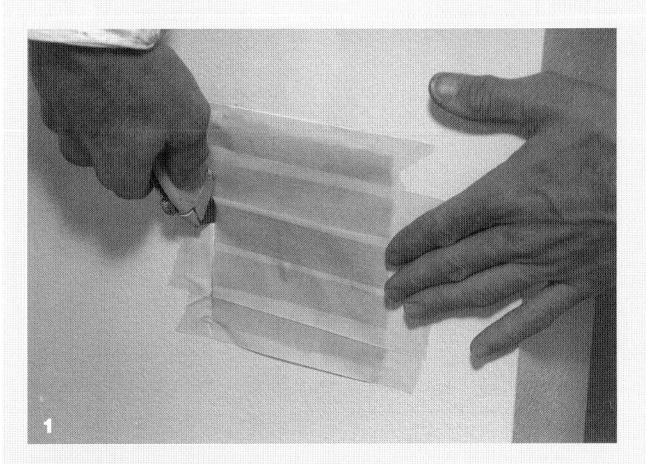
1

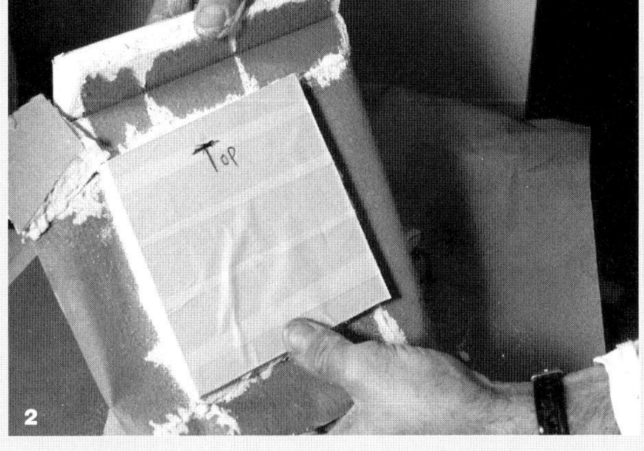

2

3

4

A work light is crucial for checking the surfaces of walls and ceilings. Aim the light across the surface to find trouble spots. Light angled this way exaggerates surface fluctuations, but you're just looking for spots that need sanding.

After repairs, sweep most of the dust off the surface, vacuum, then wipe with a damp sponge. A sponge feathers out the sanding, and the walls and ceilings will be clean and ready to prime.

Mud is actually more like paint than spackle. It has to be thoroughly mixed before you can use it. The mud might be thick, watery, or full of unmixed lumps, so stir the amount you'll need in a separate trough or bucket. A smooth consistency gives you a smoother skim coat.

The surface must be sanded and free of sanding dust for joint compound to stick. Most often a light sanding, followed by a clean damp cloth, is sufficient.

Sanding walls and ceilings

Before you can begin painting, everything you've skim-coated or patched has to be sanded. Older painted walls and ceilings seldom need much more sanding than a good feathering, or blending, of the places that have been repaired. New drywall can be "wet-sanded" with a sponge to eliminate dust, but be careful not to get the compound too wet or sponge it too much—the mud will loosen. For extensive drywall sanding, I recommend a sanding pole attached to a pivoting head that uses webbed fiberglass sandpaper. The pole greatly extends your reach and leverage, and the webbing resists clogging.

To say that sanding mud is hard and dusty work is an understatement. But if you dress for it, use a good respirator, and have the right sanding tools, you will reduce much of the annoyance (see p. 36). Keep in mind that the more even and smooth the mud is, the less sanding you have to do.

Cleaning and deglossing walls and ceilings

Regardless of what finish you plan for your top coats, you need a surface that it will stick to; painting over a dirty surface is temporary at best. Even a paint with excellent hiding properties won't stick if the surface isn't clean. The number one reason paint fails is a contaminated surface. Contaminants can be anything from dirt and dust to solvents and grease.

Kitchens often need a good degreasing, and bathrooms often suffer from mildew, so give those rooms extra attention. I prefer soap and water for interior cleaning jobs, but the build-up of grease on your kitchen ceiling may require trisodium phosphate (TSP). TSP is a caustic alkali; use gloves and eye protection.

Semi-glossy or glossy walls and ceilings need to be deglossed to give the surface some tooth (satin and flat finishes don't require deglossing). Deglossing is easy and won't leave you with a mess to clean up. You simply pour some deglosser on a clean rag—a cut-up T-shirt or other cotton cloth that won't leave lint—and wipe the entire area. You don't need to rub it in, but be careful to cover all the paint that needs deglossing. You may not see a big difference afterward, but believe me, it's there. Deglosser is available in paint and hardware stores. TSP is also a good deglosser and cleans at the same time.

All you need to degloss is a clean rag and maybe a ladder. Deglosser doesn't require much rubbing, just one firm pass over the entire area. It's a good idea to crack the window so the room can air out.

This window trim shows the stress of constant temperature fluctuations and condensation. Painting a seal around the glass will also help seal the wood.

TRIM PREPARATION

One of the first things you notice about a home's interior is the woodwork, or trim: the doors, windows, casings, and baseboards. The trim sets off the features of a room. Depending on the age and style of the house, trim may also include banisters, stairway railings, ceiling (or "picture") moldings, rafters, and mantels—any interior wood feature other than flooring. Well-kept trim can make an interior shine, but trim that is run down or peeling detracts greatly. An interior painting project presents a good opportunity to do a thorough assessment of the trim in your house.

Unless your walls and ceilings are new or recently stripped of wallpaper, the bulk of your painting preparation will be spent on the trim. You need to check

LEAD ABATEMENT

At the turn of the century, lead was mixed with linseed oil to make high-quality, long-lasting paint for all the better houses. Decades later, those houses began to deteriorate. Lead that had been dormant under layers of other paint began to deteriorate, and children living in older housing began showing symptoms directly related to lead poisoning. Legislation passed in 1971 effectively removed most lead-based paint from the market.

Lead can be ingested, breathed, and assimilated through the skin and hair. This toxic substance affects much of the body, including the blood, the reproductive and nervous systems, and the brain. Children are at the greatest risk from lead exposure, but the risk to adults can be equally lethal.

Houses built before 1978 are likely to contain some lead paint. Pre-1950s houses have the highest risk. You're involved in lead abatement any time you prep trim in an older house, so be careful. Always use a respirator—not just a dust mask.

Dry paint removal via scraping and sanding causes lead paint to disperse as fine airborne particles. Perhaps the best and safest method of lead encapsulation is a method of wet paint removal called Peel-Away that is sprayed or painted on and peeled off in thick sheets. Peel-Away comes in six systems—one for every type of job and surface. Contact your paint dealer for more information.

To obtain paint samples for lead analysis, take a utility knife and carefully cut ½-in. by 1-in. strips, leaving just a thin layer of the substrate to hold the sample together. Note the location on 5 to 10 samples from both inside and outside your house. The exterior of the house is likely to have more lead than the interior. Contact a private lab, a university extension service, or your county health department to find out where to send the samples for analysis. (*Consumer Reports* sells a video on lead-based home hazards. To order it, call 800-323-4222 or, in Illinois, 312-878-2600.)

Professional lead abatement is a serious undertaking that requires in-depth training, equipment, and health precautions. If you choose not to test your house, the safest thing is to assume that you have lead-based paint, and proceed with caution.

Here is most of the equipment you'll need for prepping trim. On wall: Tyvek painting suit. On shelf, left to right: work lights, caulk and caulk gun, sanding sponge, sandpaper, masking tape, masking dispenser, fire extinguisher, Sure-Fire torch. On ladder, top left to right: spackle, scrapers, cleaning brushes, putty knife; bottom left to right: stapler, multiple outlet adapter, foxtail broom, back-support belt. On floor, front: knee pads, dust mask; second row, left to right: work bucket, orbital sanders, gloves; rear, left to right: sanding disks, extension cord, power driver, vacuum.

the condition of the trim to find out how much prepping lies ahead, along with what tools and materials you'll need. The first place I check is the south side of the house, because southern windows suffer the most from constant exposure to sun and moisture.That's where I spend most of my time when I'm prepping an interior paint job. If the south-facing windows are in good condition, I know that the rest of the windows and trim should be in better shape and prep even faster.

Scraping paint

The primary tool I use for prepping trim is a box scraper with a carbide blade. (Note that although carbide blades are the hardest you can buy, they cannot be sharpened.) A good, sharp scraper pulls off flaking paint with ease. Less force is needed with a sharp scraper, so you're less likely to gouge the wood. Use measured, even strokes when you're scraping and try not to get carried away. Don't strip an entire piece of trim unless the paint is in bad shape. The good paint should be feathered out to match the new coats. It isn't likely that you'll have to strip all the paint down to the wood, just the cracked and peeling portions.

Stripping trim

Trim that is chipped, peeling, or covered with multiple coats will look better if it is taken down to the wood. You may find that the wood under all that paint looks better with a clear finish. Hardwoods lend warmth and charm to interiors, but stripping all the trim may require more time than you care to invest.

Tools for stripping paint include heat guns, paint strippers, and torches. I avoid using a torch on interior work because the possibility of fire damage is much greater than when I'm outside. I will use a torch if I have removed a window from its casing, because the window can be isolated on a work table.

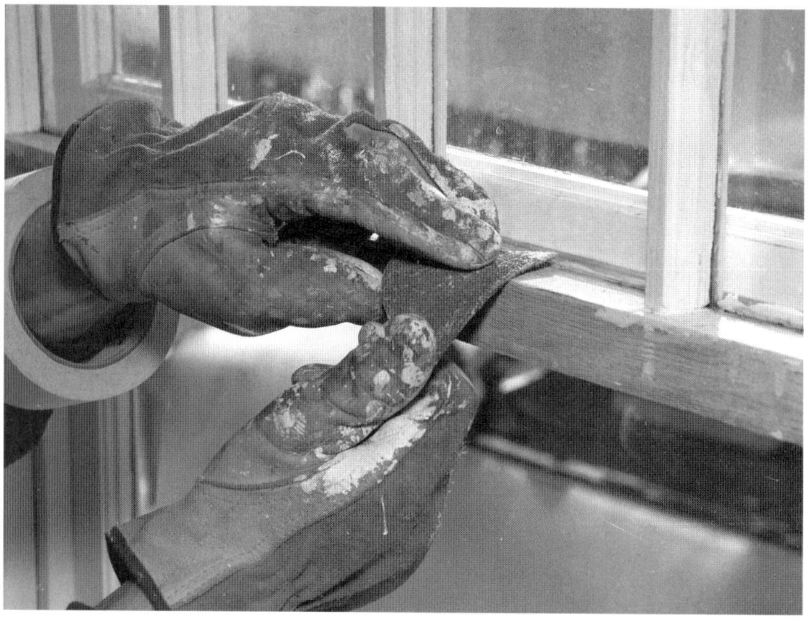

Discarded floor sandpaper is good for cutting through heavy paint build-up before you feather scraped and existing paint. Be careful not to dig into the trim.

Heat guns are slower but safer than torches for interior paint removal. Always wear protective gear, including gloves and a good respirator, when using a heat gun. Although I use a heat gun less than other methods of paint removal, these tools are less toxic than strippers, and it's always good to have a back-up. Never combine a heat gun with paint remover, which is flammable and gives off very noxious vapors if heated.

Only apply the heat gun to flat, wide areas of wood where you can peel off the loosened paint with a putty knife or scraper. Putty knives come in varying thicknesses—find a sharp one with enough stiffness to work the paint. Keep the gun moving constantly. Once the paint begins to bubble away from the wood, peel it off. Be careful not to overheat the paint, or it will turn into a sticky mess that may scorch the wood. Heat guns tend to leave more paint behind than strippers, so you need to follow up with a thorough sanding to remove any remaining paint.

Paint strippers are very good for taking trim down to the wood, but they're also highly toxic and require plenty of ventilation. Start by stripping only a 1-sq.-ft. area at a time. You can increase the area as you get more familiar with the stripper, but keep it manageable. After you've applied the stripper, wait a few minutes to let it work. A scraper, stripping brush, and toothbrush will remove most of the paint once it's dissolved. If necessary, repeat the process. Finish with #2 steel wool or a synthetic steel wool pad (which won't clog) to remove any remaining paint. Keep a container on hand for the stripped paint, as well as a bucket of warm water and a sponge. Residue left from paint strippers will keep paint or finish from adhering to wood, so thoroughly rinse the stripped areas. After the trim has dried, follow with a good sanding of 180- to 230-grit sandpaper.

Filling wood

There are lots of wood fillers and putties on the market, and you need to choose the right product for the job. Spackles are a good choice for smaller wood repairs. Wood filler is denser than spackle, less likely to shrink, and good for repairs that call for a strong binder. Because wood fillers are denser, they don't spread very easily. Wood putty is ideal for filling finish-nail holes and other areas requiring detailed finish work. Putty tends to shrink and crack less than other fillers, although I've had good experiences with newer spackles and wood fillers. Most putties can be stained—check the label to make sure (see p. 82 for how to match putty to a stained wood).

Sanding trim

After scraping, stripping, and wood filling (if necessary), I sand to feather the portions of bare or filled wood with the existing paint. If there are thick coatings of paint, I'll use a super-coarse sandpaper such as a floor-sanding grit to even out the scraped and painted areas. Stripped portions also need feathering; those areas can usually start with 180 grit.

Windows are especially prone to thick paint build-up, but regardless of how much they've been painted, window mullions and sashes require the most elbow grease—hand-sanding with sanding sponges or sandpaper. Wider areas such as window casing and baseboard (collectively called base and case) can be sanded and feathered with orbital and edging power sanders (see the photo below). Top-of-the-line sanders are worth the money—they get the job done without vibrating your hands to pieces.

Even if the existing trim finish is in good shape, you need to break the gloss with 180-grit sandpaper so the new paint can

Edge sanders are fast, time-saving tools for getting into detailed areas normally reserved for hand-sanding, such as corners, bevels, or grooves. They also save wear and tear on your wrists and fingers. Be careful when using an edge sander near glass: Keep it ½ in. away from the window to prevent scratching or breaking it.

Propping doors on stickers guarantees coverage along their bottoms.

stick well. Although deglosser can break the gloss, it won't provide the added tooth of a good sanding.

The feathering process is complete when the repairs blend into the existing paint Use your fingers to check for smoothness. Existing light can fool you into thinking everything's smooth when it's not. Remember, you don't sand trim only before you paint. For a professional finish, lighter sanding is done between coats, part of the "back-prepping" process discussed on p. 81.

Prepping doors and cabinets

Once the doors are off their hinges and labeled and the hardware is removed, I begin prepping them by stacking them on "stickers" (stakes or 2x4s) in one room or area, as shown in the top photo at left. Be careful of what you lean them against. Solid-core doors can dent walls. A length of cardboard taped behind the doors will help protect the walls.

If the doors are new or in good shape—if the finish is more or less intact—sand the door with a medium to light (180 to 220) grit of sandpaper wrapped around a sanding sponge. Most doors I come across need a few holes and nicks filled; an orbital sander speeds up the process quite a bit (see the bottom photo at left). Sand around the edges, but don't erase the identification labels on the tops.

The amount of use kitchen and bathroom cabinets get is often apparent from the traces of hand grease on their faces. Washing the cabinets will keep the sandpaper from getting clogged with grease. Cabinets that need refinishing should be cleaned before you remove them; it's faster.

After the cabinets are cleaned and dry, sand them on a work table to avoid bending over. From then on, cabinet prep is much the same as for doors and

A smooth finish requires lots of sanding between every coat. Note that even though I'm sanding outside, I'm still wearing a respirator.

Using a tack cloth

Coatings such as primer have a way of exposing every speck of dust. The importance of keeping surfaces clean cannot be stressed enough. A plain, lint-free rag is good for getting the top layer of dust, but you need a tack cloth to clean the grain and pores of sanded trim. A tack cloth will last quite a while, but if you don't refold it when it's new and after each use, it will quickly become clogged.

Tack cloths leave a thin, solvent-based residue that should be removed with a clean rag before you apply a latex or water-borne finish.

Unlike a tack cloth, a dry rag won't pick up all the dust. A rag dampened with thinner will work for general clean-up. If you use a thinner-soaked cloth for in-between sandings on finish work, make sure the cleaned area is dry before you paint it, especially if the paint is latex.

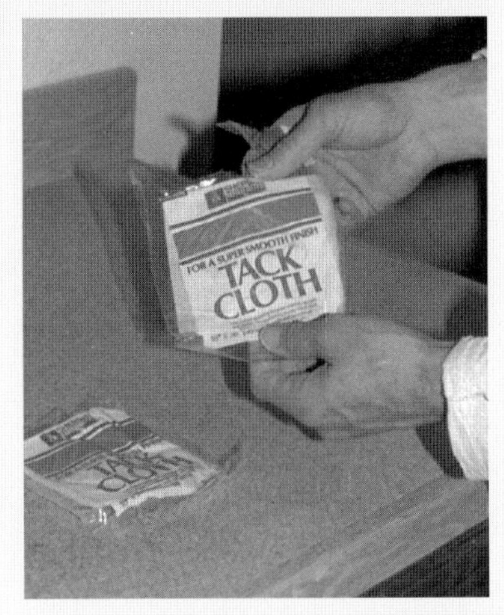

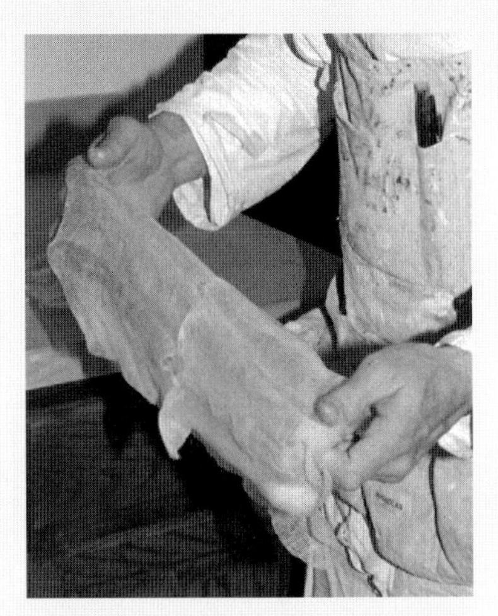

A tack cloth is an inexpensive and invaluable tool if you treat it right. Don't use it straight out of the bag—first pull it completely apart. Keep refolding the tack cloth as you use it, and before you put it away. Store it in a plastic sandwich bag to keep it from drying out.

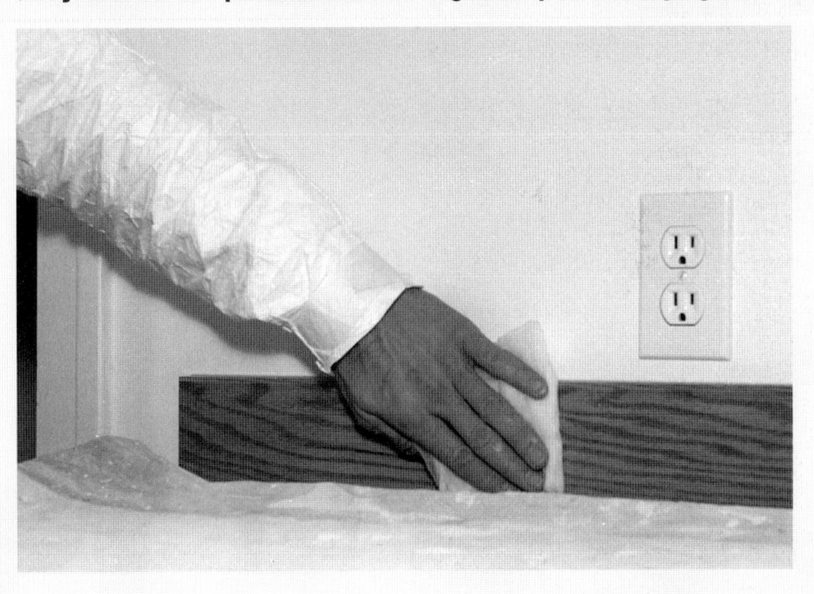

Here I'm using tack cloth to clean a recently sanded piece of trim. I also use a tack cloth before spraying or brushing a finish coat on any kind of trim.

trim. When all the cabinets are prepped and ready for paint, line them up around one room on stickers, just like the doors.

Cleaning up

As with walls and ceilings, prepped trim isn't ready to paint until it's clean. A new coat of paint on dusty trim not only looks bad but soon flakes off. And because of trim's smooth grain, any surface dust that gets in the paint is more noticeable.

Getting trim clean and ready to paint takes little more than a vacuum, a clean rag, and a tack cloth. Vacuum first, careful not to mar unfinished wood with plastic attachments. Follow by wiping the trim with a clean rag. Go over the trim once more with a tack cloth to finish (see the sidebar on p. 79).

THE INTERIOR PAINTING PROCESS

Following a logical sequence helps keep the paint job moving and mistakes to a minimum.

The sequence should begin with the ceilings, followed by the walls, then the trim. The trim is last because the walls and ceilings often are rolled or sprayed, and it's safe to assume that, even with masking, the trim will end up spattered with some paint. Trim is usually brushed, so there is less likelihood of trim paint getting on the walls. (However, if I'm painting a new house, I'll try to prime and paint the trim before it's cut and installed.)

By starting a paint stroke in the middle, I have room to move the paint. Starting in a corner with a fully loaded brush can lead to drips.

Even though trim is last in the sequence, I don't wait until the ceilings and walls are done to begin working on it. I get the trim prepped and primed before I work on the walls and ceilings. This way, the hardest part of the job is done, and any paint that spatters on the primed trim will get sanded off later.

Priming

Even walls and ceilings that are in good shape may need a coat of primer—for example, when you plan to paint a different color. Painting over a much lighter or darker color can easily take more than two coats of finish paint, but a pigmented primer that closely matches the top coat can reduce the need for multiple coats. Note that quick-drying primers like Kilz are already pigmented and can't take added pigments.

Any new or uncoated surface needs one coat of primer. Scraped and sanded trim, new drywall, and walls that have been stripped of wallpaper all need to be primed. Anywhere you've repaired holes or cracks with spackle or joint compound also will need a primer coat (this is called spot-priming, described on p. 83).

Primers are thinner than finish paints. They spread quickly and spatter easily, so be careful not to overload the brush or roller, and make sure that your masking is well-secured. A little primer goes a long way—spread it evenly. Some primers are quick-drying and set up fast, so check your work frequently for runs. Because the primer coat doesn't need to look that nice, I'm more concerned with getting it on fast, without making a mess. Finish strokes aren't a concern when priming trim; primed wood always needs to be sanded.

Accessing windows

Interior windows usually require lots of prep and priming. Your project will most likely have either a casement (or awning) window, which opens out, or an older double-hung window, which slides up.

To paint the sash of a casement window, open the window 6 in. and remove the opening mechanism. This gives you better access to the edges and frame. Paint the outer edges first, to allow more drying time. The outside edges are harder to get to when the rest of the window has been painted. Be sure to allow enough time for the outer edges to dry before closing the window, or the window will stick shut. Next, paint the sill and casing by opening the window the rest of the way. Keep the window slightly ajar to keep it from sticking shut.

When the operational part of the window is finished, paint the frame, sill, and casing. Begin the first brush stroke at the middle of the section and work the paint to the outside (see the photo on the facing page).

This stop will be replaced after the window and casing have been prepped, so I'm careful not to crack or break it trying to get it out.

Double-hung windows can be hard to access, especially where the top and bottom sashes meet. Older sliding windows often stick from too many coats of paint in the check rails, or sliders. The bottom window will slide much better when it's been taken out, prepped, painted, and reinstalled. Removing the bottom window and reaching a bare sash of the upper window takes a little carpentry and only a few minutes.

Remove one window stop from one side by scoring along the edge of the stop with a utility knife. This prevents the paint from cracking and peeling as you separate the stop from the sill and casing. Make several passes with the knife while taking care not to cut into the casing. After cutting through the paint seal, insert a putty knife or 5-in-1 scraper to loosen the stop. Pry the stop away from the casing with a wonder bar or the claw of a hammer (see the photo above). Use a small block of wood or cardboard between the pry bar and the casing to protect the casing.

With the stop removed, slide out the bottom window. A counterweight may be roped to the bottom window, keeping you from going very far. Be careful detaching the weight or it could fall and take the rope with it. When the bottom window has been removed, identify it with masking tape attached to the pane. Remember to identify the window stop, penciling the ID on its bare side. Any time a window, window stop, or other fixture is removed, be sure to identify it right away.

Holding a work light off to one side and shining it down the length of a freshly painted surface is even better than using a magnifying glass.

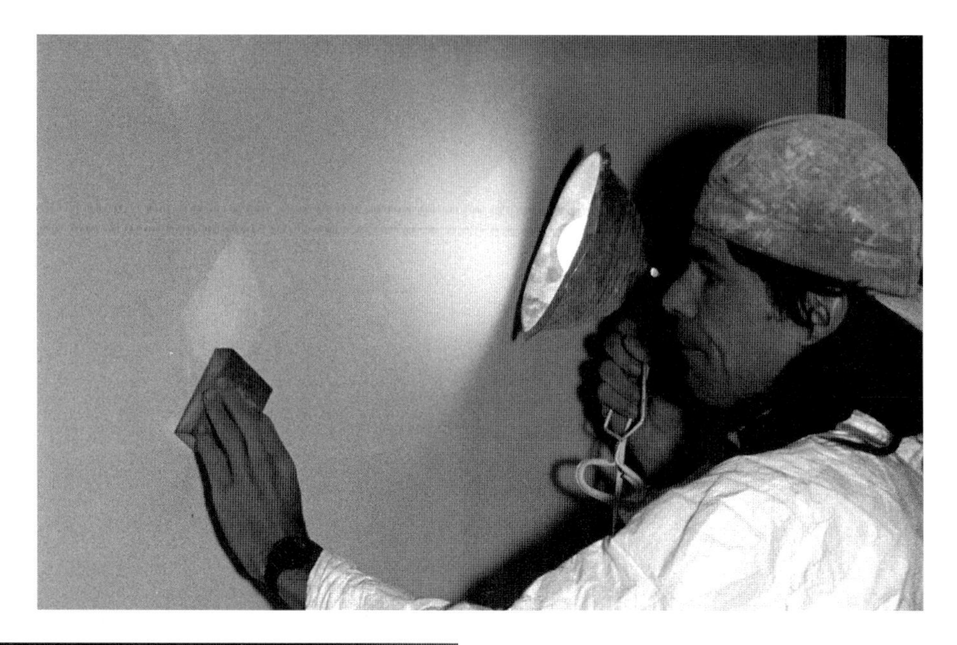

I prefer catching a run before it hardens with a lightly dampened brush. If the run has hardened, I use a sharp 5-in-1 or razor blade to slice the drip cleanly off, leaving only an outline to sand.

Use the same process to free up windows that have been painted shut. This is a common problem in colder climates, where people have tried to seal the windows against the cold.

Back-prepping

Back-prepping consists of inspecting every coat for imperfections. Most back-prepping is done after the primer coat, which highlights surface conditions. After that, there's much less back-prepping required. A portable work light is my primary tool for back-prepping; it turns up anything that shouldn't be there.

In the case of trim, or finish work, back-prepping entails lightly sanding the new primer or finish coat, and filling anything you might have missed earlier. Walls and ceilings don't need to be sanded between coats, just inspected for blemishes. Any blemishes you do find need to be fixed and sanded.

Perhaps the oldest myth concerning paint is that it covers up problem areas. Paint doesn't hide anything except the coat beneath it. In fact, paint magnifies the condition of any surface.

Spackling and sanding Any holes or blemishes that turn up with the primer coat should be lightly sanded, then filled with spackle or putty. Nail holes and other small imperfections in clear-coated (urethaned or varnished) wood trim need to be filled with a stainable wood putty. Spackle does a good job on smaller holes and blemishes on trim and walls.

Spackle and putty

Spackling small repairs like nail holes and assorted scratches in drywall and plaster is quick and easy. If applied the right way, one coat will be all you'll need. It will help if your spackle resists shrinking. Look for a top-of-the-line spackle; ask your paint dealer what brand is best (the same goes for putty).

Use your index finger to pack the spackle firmly into the surface, then make one pass over the filled area with a putty knife. This reduces the chances of shrinking and the need for another coat. Watch for any shrinkage and recoat if necessary. Follow up with a light sanding.

Getting even a close match between wood trim and wood putty used to be a hit or miss operation. After staining, the filled nail holes sometimes stood out worse than the unfilled nail holes. I've since learned that the best method is to stain the wood first, then match a putty to the stain. If you stain wood and putty at the same time, you'll probably find that they can stain quite differently. Even one length of trim might need more than one color of putty. It's a good idea to carry a palette of three or four colors of putty, just in case.

Putty tends to shrink; a second coat may be needed. A contractor friend of mine—and his full crew—once spent several days redoing every puttied nail hole in the job because the putty had shrunk.

This is a quick-drying colored putty that resists shrinking. Apply it with firm pressure in two directions, removing the extra in the second stroke.

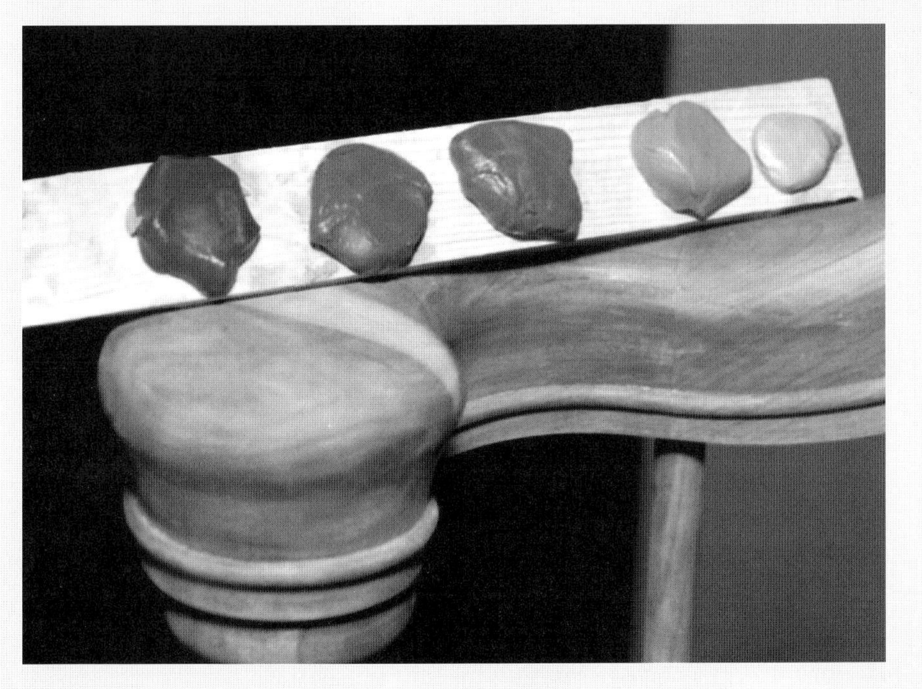

I use a mixing stick as a palette for several colors of wood putty. This piece of cherry trim has a variegated grain that needs every color of putty on my palette. Wood putty is oil-based, so I don't have to worry about the palette drying out too quickly.

Areas requiring spot-priming are usually small—all I need is a 3-in. brush. Here I'm applying stain blocker to wallpaper stains left on drywall.

Back-prepping between coats of paint includes finding and removing runs near the edges of trim, on walls, window sills, and floors. Again, use a work light to spot runs. They usually form on trim, but they can turn up anywhere. If you catch them before they've dried on oil-based paint, use a thinner brush lightly coated with thinner to feather them out. For latex paint, use a dry latex brush barely dampened with water. If you don't spot the drip until it's dried, lift it off with a 5-in-1 scraper, then lightly sand to feather it out.

Spot-priming This involves going back over the primed surfaces to check for missed areas, and priming any minor repairs you may have made. Spot-priming can reduce the need for extra finish coats on repainted trim. A single coat of primer on trim that has been selectively scraped and sanded might appear too thin; spot-priming helps blend the scraped areas and the top coat.

Spot-priming does have its limitations. The final coat might not cover the spot-primed and unprimed areas the same, leaving you with a non-uniform finish. This usually happens when you spot-prime with oil-based primer over latex paint. You may need a latex primer. In general, latex primers seem to work better at blending coats of different paint. How well a primer works also depends on how good it is. High-quality primer is worth the expense; your paint dealer can help you choose the best product.

To see how well the finish paint will react with the primed and unprimed areas, dab a small spot of paint on each area. After the paint dries, check to see if both areas have the same finish.

Caulking Although many people think it goes on before primer, caulk actually works best on top of a primer coat. Primer provides a good bonding layer for caulk. Even good caulks can shrink and leave gaps in the top coats of paint. Putting the caulk on after the primer guarantees that at least the primer will stay put.

Besides sealing the gaps around trim and windows, caulk smoothes and rounds inside edges, for easier painting and a more attractive surface. You should caulk wherever two surfaces meet at an angle, including the wood trim and walls, and wall corners (see the top photo at right).

Caulk will stretch, but don't try to caulk anything wider than ½ in. For gaps wider than ½ in., I use a polyethylene foam bead called caulk backing, then follow with a generous bead of caulk (see the photo below).

One of the last steps of surface preparation is caulking, which binds and blends the area where two surfaces meet. Sometimes caulk will shrink, making a second coat necessary.

This caulk backing worked great in filling the gap between the brick and the wall. After filling the gap with caulk backing, I finished off with a smoothed-over bead of caulk. Caulk alone wouldn't have worked in a gap this size.

I use a small piece of cardboard to scrape all the paint out of cans. This helps ensure complete mixing. When I'm finished, the can is pretty clean and ready for reuse.

Painting the top coats

Now you're finally ready to apply that new color to your wall. But first take a moment to ensure that your paint will retain its quality for future touch-ups.

Preparing the paint When I'm doing a touch-up for a client and they hand me a can with dried paint all around the edges, I know that what's inside won't be pretty. Either the paint will have dried into a hard cake or there will be a thick film on top. So I take special care whenever I open a new can of paint.

If I'm planning to reseal the can, I notch the grooved lip of the can to keep paint from drying or pooling there. I notch only one side, to keep the seal from weakening, and make a point of pouring out of that side. A well-drained lip also keeps the edge of the can free of dried specks of paint, which can end up in the brush and give the finish coat a grainy texture.

You must mix the paint thoroughly for color consistency. No matter how uniform the paint looks when you open the can, there's a good chance that some pigment has settled on the bottom. Jobs using more than one gallon of paint—especially customized paints—should be "boxed," or batched, to ensure consistent color. A 5-gallon bucket works best for batching. Mix only 3 gallons together at a time, thoroughly, before you start to paint.

Paint that has been opened and stored may oxidize, forming clumps and maybe a skin. If the skin is very thick (more than ½ in.), you should dispose of the paint. Otherwise, remove as much of the congealed paint as you can, using a stirring stick, and dispose of the clumps in a container that can be sealed and neutralized for safe disposal (see. p. 135).

After you've removed most of the lumps, there will still be smaller particles that should be strained out before you pick up your brush. Believe me, unstrained paint is a nuisance. Little clumps start showing up in your brush and everywhere you've painted.

There are two types of paint strainers: paper cones that fit a gallon can, and nylon mesh, which is often used to strain large quantities. Nylon mesh costs

Cutting in the same color on walls and ceilings is a quick process if the finishes are similar. I still try to keep the cut-in stroke fairly narrow to avoid a noticeable overlap with the rolled coat.

more, but it's reusable and it strains faster than paper cones; you can squeeze the paint through the mesh to speed it up. Make sure you have industrial-strength rubber gloves for this operation.

Cutting in This technique provides a sharp, painted border where two edges or different features meet. Trim always needs to be cut in where the wood meets another surface such as a wall or flooring. The only time you don't need to cut in is when you plan to spray your walls and ceilings. This technique is always done with a good brush that can leave a straight, sharp edge on a stroke wide enough to overlap with a roller.

The painting sequence described earlier in this chapter—ceilings, walls, then trim—also applies to cutting in. Do the ceiling first, because later you will cut in the wall to the ceiling, where any overlapping paint is less noticeable (ceilings are horizontal and don't receive as much attention as walls). If the wall and ceiling are the same color and of similar finish, you can cut in both at the same time.

To cut in trim, angle the brush so that it is almost perpendicular to the trim. This ensures a well-defined line (see the top photo on the facing page). When cutting in window glass, overlap paint 1⁄16 in. at the bottom third of the window to help seal the sash from condensed moisture.

Angle the brush as close to the wall as possible to keep the bristles from sliding off the trim.

Try to stay close to the work, whether it's near the ceiling or the floor. This isn't as comfortable as it looks.

Load less paint on your brush when cutting in trim, especially if the paint is oil-based. Try not to load more than ½ in. of the brush and slap off the extra paint. Too much paint will thicken your line and you'll lose control.

Brushing floor base and molding requires a lot of care to keep paint from dripping onto the flooring or carpet. First, pull up the floor masking tape so that none of the base is taped over. I prefer to work without an edger, but you may want to tape over the carpet if you're faced with painting over thick carpeting. However, tape isn't foolproof—don't let your line fall on it. Get as level to your work as possible; this may entail lying down next to the molding (see the photo at left). The key to getting a close, clean line is to unload the brush in a line ½ in. above the cutting edge and "coax" the paint down. If you unload too close to the edge, you'll get paint on the floor.

If you have to prime and paint bare molding above non-carpeted floor, you need to take the line right to the edge of the floor. This means you will have to clean nearly every finish stroke with a 5-in-1 tool covered with a rag. Don't use tape to mask the floor; brushed paint will get under it.

Cutting in is a little easier if the floor trim is already painted and you're going back over it with a similar color, or if the floor is carpeted. In these situations, I try to keep the cut-off point 1⁄16 in. above the floor. Getting any closer just makes for more cleanup. I prefer this technique to using a paint shield that must be cleaned on both sides after each pass.

If new carpet is being installed, take the opportunity to paint the base and molding before the carpet goes in.

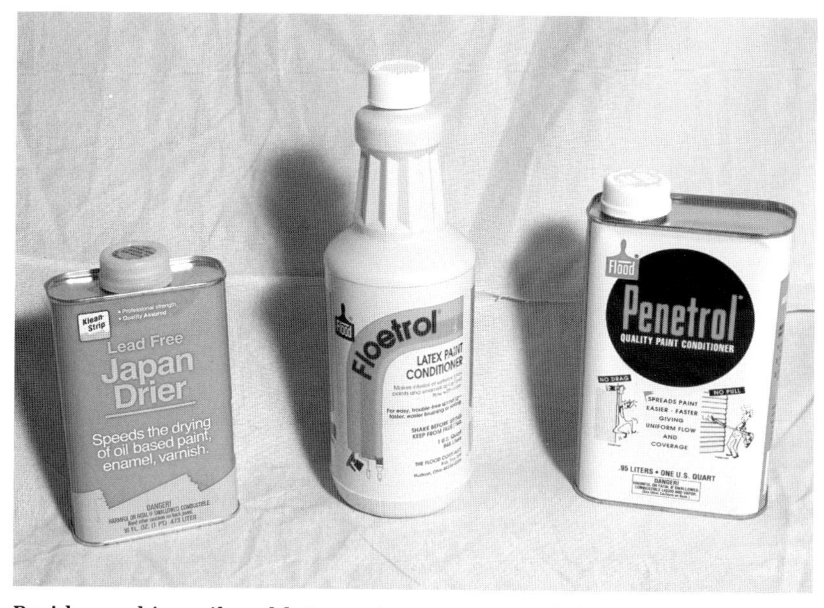

Besides making oil and latex paints more spreadable, Penetrol and Floetrol give primers better penetration on new or bare surfaces. Japan Drier can be added if you need a faster drying time between coats.

Painting doors These require at least two top coats because they are so visible. Anything less will not provide a consistent or uniform coat, no matter what the label boasts. You can use paint straight out of the can, but paint customized with either Penetrol (for oil), or Floetrol (for latex) will cover more smoothly and with much less pull, even though it has a thinner mil. "Mil" refers to the thickness of paint. Usually, two coats of paint will provide the industrial painting standard of at least five mils. However, the important factor is total paint thickness, not the thickness of each coat. In fact, three thin top coats are better than two thick top coats.

If you can choose your doors, I recommend a birch hollow-core door over a mahogany or oak door. Birch has a tighter grain and requires fewer coats of paint. Mahogany and oak take multiple coats because of their high grain structures, and their grains will always show no matter how many coats you apply. Hollow-core doors need only be painted on their sides; solid-core doors must be painted on every side to prevent warping.

If you haven't it already, raise the doors off the floor with ground stakes and rest them against a masking material. Prop the doors so that only a corner of each door rests against the wall, and pivot the doors after every coat.

Divide a door into four imaginary quarters (doors with raised panels have ready-made sections). Sectioning scales down the surface and allows you to focus your attention on one area at a time. A left-to-right pattern works best, beginning at the top. Unload the paint

A 2-in. drywall screw makes a good handle for moving a freshly painted door. Place the screw where the hinge plate was seated, or remove the middle screw if the plate is still in place.

horizontally, then spread the paint vertically with the grain. After painting two sections, feather them together before the paint sets up (you have more time to work if you're using oil-based paint). It's important to paint from the wet edge because after paint sets up, it tears instead of spreading. A paint conditioner can help you avoid tears (see p. 24).

Rolling paint on doors speeds up the process, but only use rollers on flat-surface doors. A foam rubber roller cover is ideal, but any better-quality cover will work. Roller stipple doesn't look good on doors; to feather the paint, back-brush in the direction of the wood grain. Back-brush the entire door to get a more prominent brush finish. In fact, back-brushing is a common technique for getting a smooth brush texture on wood surfaces that have been rolled and sprayed (see the top photo on the facing page).

"Drip" is one of the four-letter words of the painting business. They tend to form slowly, tricking you into thinking your job is drip-free. Drips usually form where there are surface variations, especially on edges that "knife" paint off the bristles. On doors, drips tend to form near the top and sides. This is especially true with clear finishes like urethanes and varnishes; they take longer to flash, and have more time to pool and run. Drips in clear finishes are hard to see. To prevent these little monsters from sticking, feather upward at the top of the door. Along the outside edges of the door, feather outward at a slight angle, aiming toward the ceiling. And always double-check your work.

Painting cabinet doors These must be completely sealed and finished. Their thin, solid composition makes them vulnerable to warping, and they're usually located in kitchens and bathrooms, the most humid areas in the house.

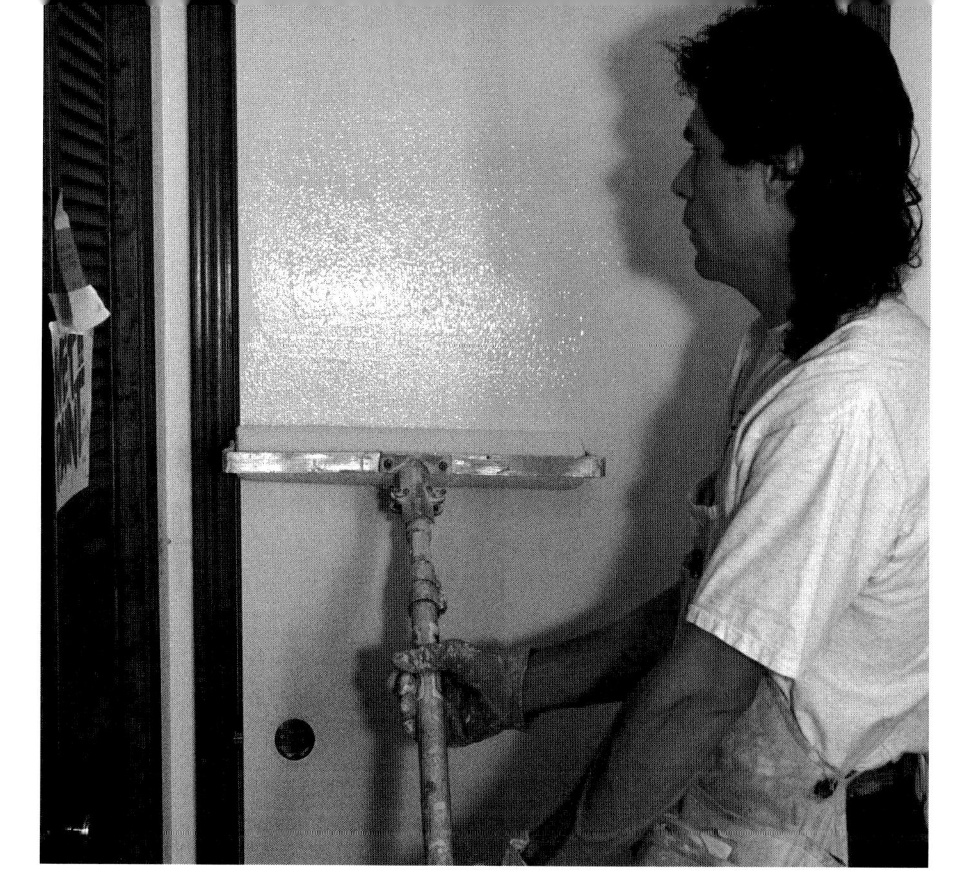

This 18-in. roller may seem like overkill, but it was already primed with the paint I needed to roll this door. Rolling flat doors is very fast. Back-brush as soon as possible—latex sets up quickly, and roller stipple doesn't look good on a door.

Although the only item in this room is a 5-gallon bucket, I make sure it's in front of me at all times. Spills are no fun to clean up, even with drop cloths.

With all their edges and corners, cabinet faces and doors demand attention to detail. You only need to cut in on the leading edges of the cabinet faces, but they are very susceptible to drips. Be sure to double-check your work. Brush finishing strokes everywhere; cabinets are very visible.

Rolling walls and ceilings Before you begin rolling, take a minute to make sure your floor and window masking hasn't torn or moved around. Always keep the roller pan, or a 5-gallon bucket with a roller screen, in front of you (see the photo at right). Backing into a pan full of paint will test not only your reflexes, but also your ability to cope with spills. (Just in case, keep lots of rags handy.)

Rolling an even, seamless coat is quite a bit more challenging than brushing. Make your first stroke a slow, upward movement to avoid dripping or spatter-

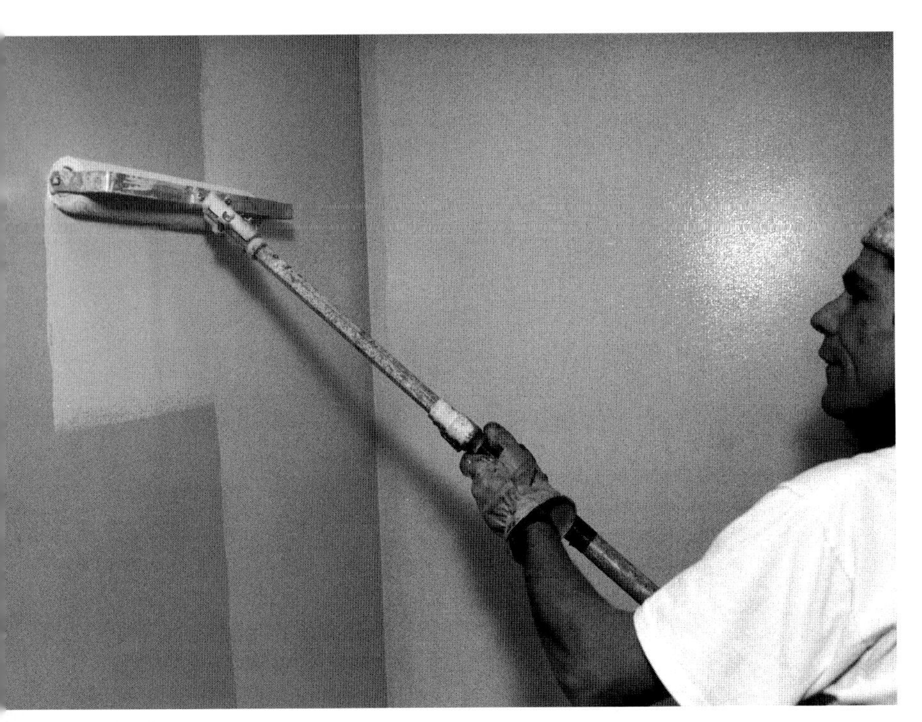

The best pattern for rolling paint is overlapping parallel strokes. The old style of zigzagging spreads paint too thin, except when you're rolling heavily textured surfaces.

ing. Quickly rolled paint spatters far and wide, and pushing a loaded roller downward guarantees that paint will drip on the floor.

When unloading your roller, use a straight-line pattern but avoid spreading the paint too thin. Newer paints can be applied much more thickly, which often allows you to cover a wall or ceiling in one coat. The old style of using a "W" or "N" to unload the roller stretches paint too thin. Roll parallel strokes, overlapping 3 in. or 4 in. with each pass. As the paint spreads out, reduce the pressure on the roller. This prevents seams from squeezing out of the roller ends. Highly textured walls and ceilings need a slightly different approach: Unload in a "W" to ensure total coverage.

Your finish stroke should be vertical and downward. Make sure to lift the roller off the wall after each stroke, for a consistent downward stipple finish. Overlap about half the cover's width in the finish stroke, using uniform light pressure and slow roller movement.

Ceilings are the most difficult surface to roll, but you can use many of the same techniques used for walls. First, band or cut in a portion of the ceiling with your roller. This frees you to concentrate on rolling the paint instead of worrying about dripping or overlapping on the walls. Unload your roller at the middle of your pattern, away from the corners, and use the parallel patterns mentioned above to spread the paint.

Make your finish stroke the width of the room. If you walk while rolling, you can roll one stroke the width of most rooms. This prevents stop-and-start seams from showing. To determine the direction of the finish stroke, find the seams in the drywall (called "flats") and follow them. However, a good drywall joint is hard to see, and you won't always have a seam to go by. Use light blending strokes in the same direction for a consistent stipple. The ceiling can be covered with one coat if it's carefully rolled with a premium paint and roller cover over the same color and finish.

Spraying interiors The pressure behind atomized spray paint keeps it airborne for a long time, especially in interiors. Masking needs to be thorough. You can minimize overspray simply by checking the masking before you spray. Working down, run your finger around the tape on the perimeter of the windows, along the molding, around door trim, along the baseboard, and over the floor masking. Overspray on finished floors and carpets can be costly, so make sure your masking is secure.

When it comes to spraying, small oversights can lead to lots of trouble. Once I sprayed several doors that I had laid out in a room. The doors and the walls were the same color, so I didn't think I needed to shield behind the doors. However, the

Banding in the ceiling with the roller is another version of cutting in. If you don't band in, you might get too much paint near an edge or corner.

Walking with a roller requires even pressure and a straight roller for the length of the stroke. It helps to hold the extension pole away from you as you walk.

walls had been painted with latex, and I was painting the doors with an oil-based finish, which oversprayed and bled through the latex. I tried to touch-up the overspray on the walls, but finally ended up respraying the entire room.

You can avoid similar problems by first determining that the wall and door paints match. The best way to see what type of paint is on the walls is to rub the surface with denatured alcohol, also known as rubbing or solvent alcohol. Oil paint will remain intact; latex will become soft and sticky (a glossy latex will resist oil bleed, however).

Follow the directions on p. 55 for using an airless sprayer. Don't skimp on protective clothing and respirators. If any part of your body is exposed, it will become covered with paint. Don't be in

Paint spray comes out at approximately 3,000 psi. It's best to move at a brisk clip to keep each coat from going on too thick.

a hurry. Once you get going there will be plenty of fast movement, so take your time when setting up the equipment.

A good place to start spraying is a closet. This lets you warm up in a place where any mistakes will be concealed. Give yourself plenty of good lighting since masked windows and paint mist will cut down on your light. Remove any obstacles and make sure your paint line is completely free—you'll have to move quickly over a lot of area. Check to be sure you have at least three gallons of paint in the sprayer bucket. Spraying uses up paint at a surprising rate. You know the paint is getting low when the pump is working hard.

Once you're comfortable using the sprayer, begin with the ceiling. Cut in a large section (or all) of the ceiling while moving at a brisk walk. Cutting in keeps you from overloading the ceiling edges. After cutting in, go back to a corner and spray the ceiling in linear strokes, overlapping as before. As with rolling, spray width-wise, using the drywall seams as a guide.

After spraying the ceiling, move down to the walls, using vertical strokes. Overlap a few inches with each pass, but don't overlap too much or you'll have uneven swaths of paint. Keep the gun going all the time on ceilings and walls, using a wrist-snap at the end of the stroke to coat the pass entirely. You'll find that a quick return motion with the gun is much faster than stopping and starting the gun with every stroke.

Most interior walls are 8 ft. high. If you're faced with walls that are out of reach, cut in the upper section using a ladder, and finish the lower section on foot. Blending upper and lower spray patterns is almost certain to require back-rolling. This step adds time to the project, but pays off in an even finish.

SPEEDING UP INTERIOR DRYING TIME

Until a coat of paint dries, your project is on hold. However, you can speed up the drying time by providing extra air flow, or exchange. This will greatly reduce the drying time, but you need to be careful about how much and when you increase air exchange in a room. The paint label will indicate the ideal temperature, humidity, and time the paint needs to dry and recoat. Try to stay close to the recommended temperature and humidity (77°F and 55% for most paints). Latex dries faster than oil-based paint.

If air exchange will lower the temperature below what's recommended for drying, first let the paint "flash," or set. Flashing means that the paint has fused to the surface without completely drying. Depending on the type of paint or finish, flashing occurs within 30 minutes to an hour after application. Flashing is critical to good adhesion. Paint that has flashed can withstand greater variations in the drying temperature and humidity.

The easiest way to get air exchange is to open doors and windows at opposite ends of the house. If it's cold or wet, turn up the thermostat to counter the cool air moving through the rooms, then open doors and windows just wide enough to promote air flow.

It's always best when spraying walls to back-roll for consistent sheen and stipple. Primer sprayed on new drywall also needs to be back-rolled, to penetrate the surface and spread any remaining drywall dust into the primer coat.

FINISHING TOUCHES

Most touch-up begins after the second (and if needed, third) top coat. Remove the masking and look for places that need a dab of finish paint. Trim edges are most likely to need touching up—check them closely. You might find nicks and scratches that occurred during the painting process, but if you were careful, touching up should be short and sweet by this stage.

Touching up also includes putting everything back in place—all the wall fixtures, outlet covers, knobs, and other hardware. Using too much force with a screwdriver can cause slips that scratch the paint. Take your time.

This wall took a beating when the new carpet went in, but Sherwin Williams professional paint does a good job of blending and hiding.

5

EXTERIOR PAINTING TECHNIQUES

The applications and techniques for interior and exterior painting are virtually identical. So is the sequence, even for masking and caulking. But the tools and methods used for preparation are very different.

Preparation is especially important when you're painting outdoors. The exterior of your house faces all kinds of weather. Sometimes paint must withstand an 80°F temperature fluctuation in a single day—and 140°F over a year. The main reason exterior paint jobs don't last is inadequate preparation. Sanding—rather, the lack of it—is the main culprit. Every type of exterior surface requires slightly different prep.

However, poor preparation isn't the only reason that exterior paint and stain give out. A poor quality of primer and top coat will hasten paint failure. Temperature and humidity also are important factors that influence how well paint sticks to a surface.

EXTERIOR SURFACE PREPARATION

The key words to remember for properly prepped exterior siding are clean, dry, and dull. If the surface that you're about to coat with paint or stain fits that description, then it's ready for paint. Let's start by talking about cleaning.

Cleaning techniques

Making sure the siding is clean and ready to paint is usually the easiest part of exterior prep. After I've scraped and sanded, I sweep all prepped areas with a foxtail broom. A thorough sweeping is all that most siding needs for prep, if siding is in good shape (and there's no scraping or sanding needed).

Sometimes, though, you have to wash the siding. There are several methods, but whatever you do, never wash wood siding that's been scraped and sanded—water will roughen up the feathered edges of the paint.

Soap and brush "Keep it simple" is a constant refrain in the building trades, and cleaning techniques are no exception. The easiest and most economical method for cleaning siding is to use a garden nozzle and long-handled car brush. I spray the siding with water, then brush it with a mild detergent.

Whenever you use water for cleaning and prepping, make a point of washing early in the morning so the surfaces have all day to dry out. I allow at least 24 hours for wood to dry before I resume prepping and priming it.

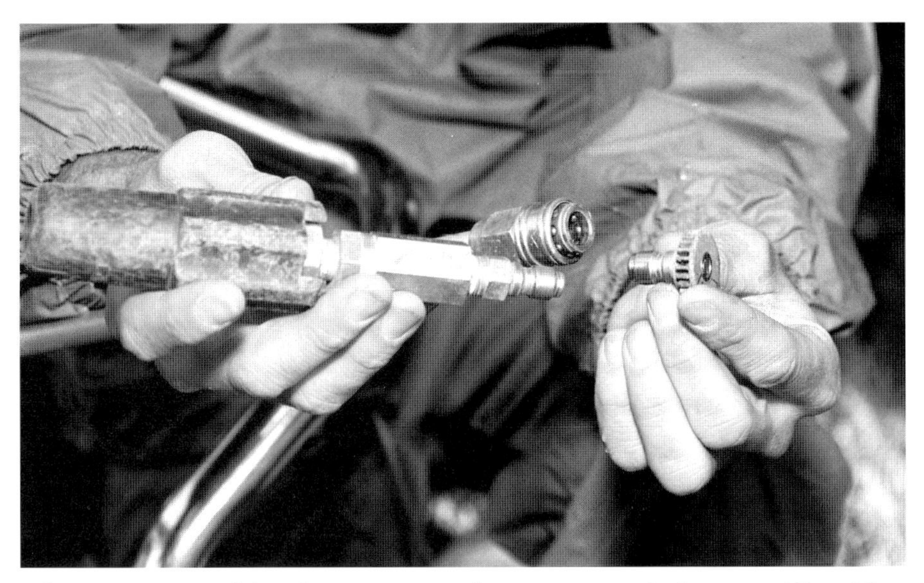

When pressure washing, be sure to use the correct nozzle for your siding. The nozzle on the left is a pulsating nozzle good for washing masonry, but it destroys wood. The nozzle on the right can be used for non-masonry siding.

Pressure-washing the entire side of this house took only 20 minutes. A car-washing brush with an extension handle also would have worked on this redwood, but it would have taken more time and effort.

Pressure washers Pressure washers are powerful cleaning tools, but they cannot be used on every type of siding. Older houses with little or no insulation should never be power-washed. Once water gets between the siding and the walls, dry rot sets in. I also avoid power-washing stucco: one too-close swipe and the stucco flies off. Ditto for log houses, even if they appear to be well-chinked. Logs tend to split, and the water will take forever to dry out before you can go back and coat the logs. Siding shingles are another vulnerable surface—it doesn't take much water pressure to loosen or blow them right off the wall.

Pressure washers tend to pit wood and crush wood fibers, reducing the wood's ability to adhere to paint or stain. Their high pressure tends to force water through seams in the siding, such as the bottom edges under lap siding, so avoid pointing the nozzle upwards, and keep the spray tip away from roof shingles. Be careful not to set the pressure too high; start low and adjust upward if necessary.

Pressure washers can be dangerous on window and door trim. A direct blast of water will break a window, and it's easy to get water between the trim and siding unless the seal is nearly perfect. Always back up an extra 2 ft. or 3 ft. around any trim. I once worked with a paint company that didn't back off around trim. The apparatus we used had so much force that one person had to stay on the inside of the house to mop up water that sprayed through the window casings.

I know I've made pressure washers out to be lethal weapons, but on the right siding—and in competent hands—power-washing can be a good method of cleaning siding. Pressure washers are very effective for blasting off old paint and moss, exposing weak areas of paint that otherwise might not be seen, and cleaning off residue such as chalk and efflorescence. You may even find that a good power-washing is all that your house needs to look better (assuming there's no peeling or blistered paint).

Using pressure washers

Protect yourself well when operating a pressure washer. These powerful tools send paint chips flying, and the spray alone can cause injury. Wear face protection and rubber gloves. If you need to be on a ladder, make certain that you and the ladder have solid footing and that you have a good grip—a pressure washer can knock you off your balance.

Pressure washers rent for $50 to $75 a day. Most washers have variable pressure, usually from 1000 to 2500 psi. Keep the pressure at or below 2000 psi to keep surface damage to a minimum. You can also vary the pressure by moving the spray wand closer to or farther from the surface. The fan of spray should be between 6 in. and 1 ft. from the surface to be most effective, especially for removing loosened paint. If the wood is covered with paint or stain, hold the tip 6 in. to 8 in. from the surface. If the wood is bare, keep the tip about 1 ft. away. (Closer spray may damage uncoated wood.) Pressure washers don't remove spider webs or cocoons very well, so don't keep going over an area trying to dislodge them—it's better to use a wire brush or scraper.

Before you get started with a pressure washer, take a few minutes to cover the ground where you'll be washing. Paint flakes and chips are a nuisance to clean up, especially if the ground is wet. Your drop cloth only needs to catch loose material that comes off the siding, so anything from plastic to cardboard works fine.

Brace yourself before pulling the trigger on a pressure washer—they can knock you off-balance. Good rain gear and goggles make the job easier.

I cover the area I'm pressure-washing with cardboard. Cardboard is more portable than canvas and absorbs more water. Drop cloths tend to get soaked.

As with any new piece of equipment, begin your initiation to a power washer on a less-visible section of your house. Move the wand in the direction of the siding or wood grain. Avoid aiming the washer up or under the siding. Not only does water take forever to dry out under siding, but if it runs out after you've painted, the paint may run. Never underestimate the harmful potential of water.

Try adding a small amount of all-purpose cleaner to the water to remove hard-to-wash deposits such as chalking or grime. Before you go to the trouble of adding detergent to a pressure washer, first try plain water with a mild pressure of 1200 to 1500 psi. Never add mildewcides or other caustic cleaners to a power washer solution—they can hurt both you and the equipment.

A pressure washer can be of most help on masonry, vinyl, metal, and rough woods like cedar and redwood. Barns and sheds are good candidates for power washing; their thin, uninsulated walls can dry thoroughly. When I'm deciding whether to power-wash wood, I first check the vapor barrier under the siding. Foam vapor barriers such as Celotex have an efficient, aluminum-like skin. Many other houses have Tyvek under the siding. Tar paper is less of a vapor barrier than a water-proofing skin for the sheathing beneath the siding. In these cases, power-washing can work well.

Wood cleaners Wood cleaners are very good for bringing old wood back to life. They remove old oxidized layers of coatings like semi-transparents, solid oil stains, and clear finishes. Bio-Wash, Okon Wood Cleaner, CitrusSolve, and Olympic Deck Cleaner are four biodegradable cleaners. Most of these products provide complete systems for cleaning decks, restoring weathered wood, and stripping failed stains and clear coatings (see Resources on p. 144).

One reason I prefer using these cleaning products is that their active ingredient, oxalic acid, is easy on the environment. Other wood cleaning systems use a diluted version of methylene chloride, the main component of paint strippers; it breaks down into "gray water safe" residue. Gray water needs to be treated at a waste-water plant, so don't pour these cleaners down storm drains or into open water. (See Chapter 6 for more information on waste and safe disposal.)

Wood cleaners are easy to apply and rinse. The more caustic wood restorers and stain strippers require some scrubbing to get down to bare wood. If your siding has what is known as a "heavy build," or thicker clear coats that show signs of failing such as yellowing, cracking, or peeling, then brace yourself. Heavy-build coats can take up to three coat-and-rinse cycles with even the best wood restorers to get down to bare wood. I know that sounds like a lot of time, money, and effort just to get siding clean, but the fact is there really aren't many alternatives.

Prepping a deck is easy if it's in good shape. I spray the deck with water, scrub it with Bio-Wash (or similar biodegradable deck cleaner), then rinse. A clean deck has a more uniform surface and will stain more evenly.

Unlike interior varnishes and lacquers, exterior clear coatings are too soft to sandblast. A paint dealer I know once ordered several gallons of a popular wood cleaner/restorer for a contractor who balked when he realized he would have to use multiple applications to remove a heavy-build clear coating. The contractor decided it would be faster to sandblast it instead. He ended up with a painter's nightmare. The soft coating sandblasted unevenly and the wood was destroyed in the process.

There are two morals to this story. The first and most obvious one is face up to the necessary work and do it right. Secondly, there are ways to keep future prep work to a minimum. When you select the next coating for your house, consider the maintenance involved. Ask yourself (and your paint dealer) what you can expect down the road from a

This shows dried mildew in a basement apartment. Moisture from the adjoining bathroom migrated into the bedroom, giving mildew a foothold. A concentrated bleach and mildew-cleaning solution—and repairs in the bathroom—took care of the problem.

particular type and brand of paint or stain, and the best ways to make it last. Yearly cleaning or recoating is often the recommended maintenance for many exterior coatings.

Mildewcides Mildew is a mold that's common in humid and shady areas of the house. You can tell mildew from dirt by applying diluted bleach. Bleach kills fungus on contact—if the darkened spot begins to disappear, it is mildew and needs to be addressed. If the bleach just runs down the siding, you're looking at dirt (see Resources on p. 144).

Top-of-the-line paints have built-in mildewcides, but these only inhibit mildew growth. They won't get rid of existing mildew (highlighting the need for thorough prep). You can add mildewcide to the paint itself, but be careful. Mildewcides are toxic and should be handled with care.

Most paint manufacturers have a separate mildewcide cleaner that you add to bleach for a sure-fire cleaning solution. Pittsburgh Paints makes a very good cleaner called Mildew Check that not only removes mildew and algae, but also leaves a protective coating that inhibits any comeback attempts. Remember always to protect your face, eyes, and skin when working with mildewcides, and dispose of them properly. As with any new or unfamiliar product, read and follow the directions carefully. Mildew cleaners can be painted over after they have dried for 24 to 48 hours.

In regions with high humidity, I recommend keeping trees and shrubs a couple of feet away from the siding, especially in shaded areas. It's also a good idea to keep the siding clean with yearly maintenance—for instance, a washing in the dry part of summer, when the siding can quickly dry out.

New wood siding

New building materials are constantly coming on the market, but wood is still the most popular siding. Wood exteriors vary quite a bit. Older houses usually have lapped siding, while some newer homes have hardboard siding with embossed grain. There is also log, cedar, and redwood siding, paneling, and shingle siding. The nature and characteristics of each kind of wood determine how you prep it.

Cleaning new wood New wood siding might appear ready to be painted, but look closely. Studies show that a mere two weeks can weather wood enough to hurt paint's ability to stick to it. The best way to take off the weathered layers is to sand or brush the siding lightly, clean it with a stiff bristle broom, then follow with a foxtail brush. To get the siding really clean, use compressed air to blow dust and dirt out of all the wood pores (contractors don't usually go to that much trouble). You can tell if new siding is clean by running your hand over the surface to check for dust or chalking (see p. 115).

Back-priming new wood Vapor barriers on most newer houses reduce much of the migration of moisture through the walls. Older homes often have no vapor barrier at all. However, unless the house is super-insulated with a 3-in. vapor barrier, there will always be moisture moving out of the house through the siding. Once that happens, the paint or stain starts to blister or peel. Giving siding its own vapor barrier is the best protection.

Coating each piece of siding with paint or stain is called back-priming, or prepriming. (Back-priming also means touching-up to make sure that all bare surfaces are covered with primer, as discussed on p. 84.) If you recall from earlier chapters, priming serves several functions, the most important being to seal a surface. Back-priming a piece of siding simply means priming all four sides, leaving the ends unsealed. You have to leave the ends unsealed because the siding often still has to be measured and cut, and even cured wood still contains some moisture that needs to escape.

You're lucky if you're able to prime and seal the siding before it goes on the house. In the process you'll add years of life to the paint job and the wood. You'll spend more time and money to seal all around the siding, but this investment will pay off for years. If you're painting the siding, you only need to seal it with primer; I recommend two coats. Exterior stains and clear coatings have their own built-in sealers and can be used to back-prime.

If you own a sprayer, spraying is the quickest method of back-priming siding. Siding that's been laid out to dry takes up a lot of room, and you probably won't be able to spray it all at once. Spraying in batches is time-consuming and makes renting a sprayer too costly.

Wood bleeding and lumber treatments

Kiln drying is part of the wood-curing process; some, but not all, of the moisture is heat-forced out of the wood. This process forces sap to the surface, usually to the knots. Look for signs of bleeding in the lumber you buy. Before you can paint, you need to seal knots, and any other places showing bleeding, with a stain blocker, or a primer/sealer with shellac.

Lumber companies coat wood with several types of treatments, depending on the type of wood and where it's going. For example, southern pine gets more stabilizing and termite-resistant coatings than wood cut in the West. These treatments include water-repellent wax, fungicides, water-borne salts, and coatings designed to disguise the appearance of certain woods. All such treatments adversely affect the sticking power of paint or stain.

Most wood treatments weather away after a few weeks. You can speed the process by pressure-washing or using a wood cleaning system such as Bio-Wash or CitrusSolve. If you're still concerned about adhesion, sand and coat the wood with a high-end sealer before you paint.

This redwood siding is back-primed with the ends left unsealed to let moisture escape. Although I used a 4-in. China bristle brush for this example, I would spray if the project involved lots of new siding.

I begin scraping siding with a sharp box scraper. Always wear eye protection and gloves when scraping.

A more economical way to back-prime siding is to roll on at least one thick coat of primer—two coats are even better. When back-priming, be careful to make sure the bottom edges of the siding are well-coated. The bottom edge is where rain, ice, and dew gather, and if it isn't sealed, water will do a number on the siding. Even hardboard siding such as Colorlok delaminates if water seeps in through the bottom edge.

Painting new wood Rolling on the primer and the top coats is plenty fast, and there's less overspray and waste than with spraying. If you roll, be certain to back-brush the side that will be exposed. Back-brushing (see p. 52) smoothes out the stipple left by rollers.

Whenever you are back-brushing or back-rolling, remember not to get too far ahead of yourself as you apply the paint. Roll the siding for a minute or two, then quickly back-brush it. Latex sets up faster than oil-based paints, and if you get too far ahead of yourself, you'll end up tearing it. Keep in mind that you can roll much faster than you can brush. If possible, keep the siding out of direct sunlight when you're painting.

Old wood siding

Older siding usually needs more than just a cleaning. Unless the exterior has been very well maintained over the years, count on hitching up your sleeves for several rounds of scraping, sanding, priming, and caulking. Those four steps are the sequence for prepping most older wood siding, including poplar, pine, cedar, redwood, and hardboard.

Scraping old wood There are a few important points to keep in mind when you're scraping the exterior. First, use drop cloths under your work area. Second, keep your scraper blade sharp, and don't hesitate to stop to sharpen it when you notice yourself having to work harder. Finally, don't spend more than a few hours scraping and sanding, since you'll need to prime what you've scraped before the day is over. If you don't, you'll find yourself having to resand what you sanded the day before. Remember this formula: three hours of prepping to one hour of priming.

For smaller touch-up jobs, I use a 5-in-1 or putty knife to scrape off the peeling paint (left), then I smooth the edges with a fast-drying spackle (right) and sand with an orbital sander. I use this method only for touch-ups, not for siding that needs major preparation.

After I've gone over the worst areas with the scraper, I begin feathering them with a shave-hook scraper and propane torch. (If you don't have a shave-hook, a regular box scraper will do.) Combined, these tools loosen the more ragged edges of paint as well as stubborn clumps that form. This is an important step in siding prep; torching and scraping make feathering with a sander much easier. Torches are also great for knocking cocoons and spider webs off the eaves.

Practice using a torch and scraper in a less visible area until you feel comfortable using the tools together. Use a low heat setting on the torch and hold it a few inches away from the paint. Move the torch back and forth over one area until the paint begins to bubble up. Scrape the heated paint away from the torch to avoid burning your hand. Move the torch steadily, taking care not to

This Sure-Fire propane torch has a triggered igniter for greater control. Note that I'm wearing a respirator for protection from fumes. Fumes from burning paint are extremely toxic.

This side of a garage is the average square footage for a full day of prepping. Use a ratio of three hours of prep to one hour of priming (with a brush) to estimate how much time you will need.

overheat the paint. Even though I move the torch pretty fast, I know that there is always going to be some scorched wood that I can sand later with an orbital sander.

Important: If you are torching the paint on a very old house, check to make sure that newspaper wasn't used for insulation. Newspaper was commonly used to insulate before building codes took effect, and quite a few older houses still contain it. If you aren't sure, you can always use a heat gun. It's slower than a torch, but you'll get the same results.

Sanding old wood I finish feathering the scraped areas with a power sander, such as a random orbital, and a medium grit of sandpaper. If you're facing extensive exterior prep work and don't own an orbital sander, I strongly advise renting one. The top coats of paint will look much better once the scraped and existing paint have been finely blended together. Don't forget, new coats of paint emphasize any irregularities left by the sanding and scraping process.

Priming determines the strength of the top coats. Use a high-end latex or oil-based primer, and double-coat where extra protection is needed.

Priming old wood Once all the siding has been scraped, sanded, and swept clean, I prime it with a high-quality exterior primer. For trouble areas that need extra protection, I add Penetrol or Floetrol to the primer (see p. 24). More humid conditions and regions of the country often demand two coats of primer for extra bonding. You also should consider double-coating the siding with primer if your paint job entails extensive repainting.

Keep in mind the need to bring all the surfaces up to par, which means matching the prepped siding to the existing paint in appearance and quality. One good primer coat and two top coats should be enough to match most siding jobs.

The primer can be rolled or brushed on. I generally use a 4-in. China bristle brush for spot-priming. A 4-in. brush allows me to reach nearly everywhere: under eaves, soffits, and the bottom edges of the siding. Rollers come in handy if there is a lot of siding to prime. They apply a thicker coat, and I advise a thick coat of primer, especially if you're just applying one coat. If you roll the primer, use a roller cover that is the width of the siding, and back-brush to remove the stipple. Avoid rolling with a 9-in. roller on a ladder—it will wear you out. A 6-in. Long Reach roller assembly is much lighter and easier to maneuver on a ladder. A 6-in. Long Reach will easily fit inside a 5-gallon bucket suspended from a ladder rung.

Don't prime too early or late in the day, or the primer might be affected by dew or falling temperatures. Make sure the wood is completely dry and clean.

Thoropatch is an excellent product for repairing masonry. A peanut-butter consistency spreads and sticks best (left). A sponge trowel textures the Thoropatch to match the stucco (right). The trowel should just be damp: Too much water in the sponge will smear the patch.

Stucco

Stucco is highly textured and tends to hold dirt. You can remove a light layer of dust with just a hose and nozzle, but thicker accumulations of dirt require more cleaning. The heavy texture of stucco makes it hard to clean with anything other than a stiff brush such as a long-handled car-washing brush. (Unless the stucco is in near-perfect condition, avoid pressure-washing it.) Wet the stucco down, then brush it with detergent, and finish with a good rinsing. While cleaning the stucco, check for cracks that need repairing.

Once the stucco is clean and dry, you need to repair any cracks. Caulking is the easy solution, but caulk dries to a different sheen and definitely has a smoother texture than stucco. This makes getting a good match difficult. However, you will need to caulk where there are gaps between the trim and the siding (see p. 124).

I use Thoropatch, a masonry patching product. I mix the Thoropatch with its acrylic additive in a 5-gallon bucket, then apply the mixture with a 6-in. broad knife much the same way I fill drywall cracks (see p. 70). I texture the repair with a dampened sponge trowel; if you don't have a sponge trowel, you can use a damp sponge to texture the patch. Prime the patches with a recommended stucco (masonry) primer when they have dried.

Priming and sealing stucco is critical in getting the stucco to last, especially in colder regions. Stucco is fairly porous and if water gets inside it and freezes, cracking will occur. The type of primer you use for masonry surfaces like stucco depends on the condition of the surface. Older stucco can be primed with everything from latex paint to varnish sealers to alkali-resistant primers. Okon has a line of masonry sealers and stains that I've yet to try, but comes highly recommended.

Newer stucco has a high alkalinity that requires a primer like Pittsburgh's Speedhide Alkali Resistant Primer or a quality sealer such as Sherwin Williams's Loxon or Okon masonry sealers.

It's a good idea to top-coat stucco (and most other types of masonry) with latex, which does a better job of sticking to hard, porous surfaces than oil-based paints. I use latex mixed with Emulsabond for a primer (see p. 24). However, you can dispense with painting new stucco altogether if you color the stucco when it is first mixed and applied. Providing the color mixtures are even, you'll have the color you want without any of the hassles of painting it later.

Vinyl siding

If you're painting over vinyl siding, chances are that it hasn't been painted before. That's why most people use vinyl siding: It supposedly never needs painting, although it will fade. But you may want to paint vinyl to change the color.

Prepping vinyl siding is much the same as prepping wood. Make sure the surface is clean, dull, and dry. The dull part is what should concern you; vinyl siding has a smooth surface. No matter how good the paint, it can't stick to a surface that has no grip. You'll need to roughen smooth siding with a fine grit of sandpaper, then sweep or wash it. I recommend spraying or power-washing non-porous siding materials such as vinyl because they can't absorb moisture and will dry fast.

Olympic Vinyl and Wood Siding Wash is good for washing virtually any type of siding. This is a non-scrubbing wash that you apply with a garden sprayer and rinse off with water. The active ingredients are non-toxic solvents that are gray water safe (see p. 99).

The primer you use on vinyl doesn't need to seal it, only stick to it. Use latex paint with Emulsabond for extra adhesion. It is important never to apply a color that's darker than the original vinyl color. The paint will expand and contract more than the vinyl, and have trouble sticking. Make sure you paint vinyl the same or a lighter color.

Aluminum siding

Aluminum also needs to be clean, dry, and dull before priming, but because aluminum is a metal there can be other considerations as well. Most new, unpainted aluminum can simply be cleaned and primed with a metal primer such as Pittsburgh's Zinc Chromate Primer or Sherwin Williams's Direct-To-Metal (DTM) Acrylic Bonding Primer. The metal must be completely clean before priming. Metal has minute pores that give siding some tooth, but grease, rust, oil, and dirt can fill these pores and almost repel paint before it dries. And rust left beneath a coating of paint will continue to grow, eventually forcing paint off the surface.

New aluminum siding often has a rust-inhibitor that needs to weather over time. Some paint manufacturers recommend not painting new aluminum or vinyl siding, in order to let it weather. Some aluminum is coated with corrosion-resistant materials, such as Duranar, which require special primers. Here's how to identify Duranar: Scrape away the coating, and if you see yellow primer below, it's Duranar. Pittsburgh Paints recommends more than 10 primers you can use for Duranar, including Pitt-Guard Direct-To-Rust and All-Weather Pitt-Guard Direct-To-Rust. Other coatings include Teflon and Kynar. Check with your supplier for special painting recommendations for new siding.

It's very important that aluminum siding be thoroughly sanded and prepped before you attempt priming and topcoating it. Sandblasting will make short work of the sanding job, but the sand will make short work of your flower beds. You may find a sandblaster that blends water with the sand to reduce dust, but those types of blasters are rare. Silica dust isn't a very healthy substance; complete protective gear is advised. Wait for a perfectly still day, then mask off nearby windows and cars (if silica dust gets on any glass or windshields, wash it off quickly or the dust will ruin the glass). Then hire someone for the job—sandblasting is nasty work.

Aluminum siding that is already painted also will need sanding, although not as much as some of the newer aluminum siding. Bear in mind that there is a difference between exposed and unexposed aluminum siding. Exposed siding is likely to have a chalky residue as well as dirt and, in more humid environments, mildew. Power-washing-exposed siding will eliminate much, but not all, of the residue and dirt. Weathered aluminum will require additional scrubbing with a car-washing brush to remove chalking. Remove any mildew with the mildewcides mentioned on p. 100. After the siding has dried, run your hand over it. You'll probably still see some residue, but don't expect to remove all of it. In these cases you should prime the siding with an extra-sticky primer, such as a Direct-To-Metal (DTM) by Sherwin Williams, Speedhide zinc chromate primer by Pittsburgh, or Suprime 9 by Pratt & Lambert. As mentioned previously, add Emulsabond if you use latex, or Penetrol for oil primers, because aluminum is smooth and demands maximum adhesion.

Less-exposed aluminum siding on the eaves, porches, and soffits is often intact and easier to prep. All those areas need is a good power-washing or dousing with a garden hose, followed by a sweeping of cobwebs and cocoons.

Keep your eye on the weather and temperature. Metal siding is very sensitive to temperature and humidity changes that can ruin a good paint job.

Steel siding

The preparation for steel is very similar to aluminum, with some differences. Steel tends to rust and corrode more than aluminum, so prep sometimes calls for more grinding or sandblasting. Steel siding may have a protective coating of grease or oil that must be removed. If any existing coating is glossy, give it a light sanding or deglossing to dull the finish. Pre-painted steel siding will likely have some flaking paint that needs scraping and sanding, followed by a thorough dusting. Remove all the rust you can with a sander. Carefully clean the rusted sections and prime them right away. Any grease or oil stains also need to be cleaned; use denatured alcohol, ammonia, or a strong detergent. Rinse the siding well and let it dry completely before you prime it. Steel can be primed with a rust inhibitor such as Sherwin Williams's DTM Acrylic or Pittsburgh's Rust Inhibitive Primer.

Prime and paint steel siding early in the day, after it's had time to warm up. Don't attempt to paint steel or aluminum siding if there is a chance that the temperature will drop. I once tried beating the weather on a large commercial building. The temperature dipped below 45°F that night, before the paint had time to dry, and by the next day most of the coating had sagged (see p. 116). I spent the next five days using paint removers and sanding to get back to square one. So take it from me: You should paint only the amount of siding that you know can dry before the temperature dips or the weather changes.

Galvanized steel siding

You need to exercise care with galvanized steel siding. If the siding is already painted, then obviously it's fine to repaint it after the usual cleaning and prepping. Even with pre-painted siding you have to check carefully for rust and remove as much of it as you can. Spot-prime with a rust inhibitor. Galvanized steel should also be cleaned with thinner. The old school of thinking was to clean galvanized steel with vinegar, but acid washes have been found to pit the galvanizing layer and weaken the paint.

If the galvanized siding hasn't been painted, you need to determine if you can paint it. The best way to find out is to ask your supplier if the metal has been treated. Some galvanized steel is coated with a stabilizer that prevents white rust from forming. Stabilizers don't weather or wash off, and painting over them is close to impossible. You can remove the stabilizer by sandblasting it or using a powerful solvent. However, leaving unpainted galvanized steel alone might be the best course to take.

I know of only one primer made specifically for galvanized steel: Pittsburgh Paint's Speedhide Galvanized Steel Primer. You can also use the primers listed on p. 27. Alkyd primers aren't recommended because their fatty acids form a soap that causes the primer to lose its adhesion. Stick with latex primers when working with galvanized steel.

Concrete and masonry

Exterior concrete left unpainted or unsealed is fair game for the elements. Weathering eats away at even the hardest concrete over time, and small cracks form and spread. Foundations crack under stress. Freeze-thaw cycles add to

To remove the 15 layers of paint on these concrete steps, I smooth on a coating of Peel-Away with a small applicator and a trowel (left). It's important to apply the Peel-Away cloth carefully and smooth out air bubbles. A 3-in. scraper is necessary to lift Peel-Away off the concrete (right). Although Peel-Away does a great job of loosening the paint, I still need to scrape, wire brush, and thoroughly wash the area with lots of water.

the damage: Water acts like miniature wedges in the concrete, widening cracks. These fissures have to be repaired or they'll get bigger. Once the masonry is repaired and prepped, a coating such as latex paint, stain, or sealer will keep masonry intact.

Prepping masonry Concrete is basically the same material as stucco, but the texture is different and so is the painting preparation. New and unpainted concrete usually has to cure for 90 days before you can paint it, although there are several products now available that can be applied with much less curing time. Pittsburgh Paints recommends 30 days before using their masonry primers, but companies including Sherwin Williams and Okon claim only seven days of curing are enough for their sealers. Concrete (and masonry like brick and block) has to cure so the alkali and moisture can leach out. New concrete has form oil on the surface that must be removed along with any additives that might have been used to speed up the curing process.

Stripping and etching masonry One of the best new methods for skinning paint off masonry is the Peel-Away system. Peel-Away has revolutionized paint removal with the creation of a brush-on system that anyone can use. This system also makes paint removal safer, by encasing each layer of paint in a blanket that is peeled off, eliminating potentially hazardous paint dust, including lead (see p. 75).

Peel-Away is very good for removing coatings of paint from detailed surfaces, from brick to interior fireplace mantels. Peel-Away is also used to strip coatings from large areas such as walls and floors (smaller, more confined areas should be stripped by hand). A brush, roller, or small plastic applicator is all you need to apply the residential version of Peel-Away (#6). A thin fabric is then placed over the coated area to keep it moist and bind the coating together, so you can peel off the layers of paint (see the photos on p. 109).

Sandblasting is one way to remove oils, grease, or additives, and give new concrete some grip in the process. Sandblasting is also good for removing crumbling masonry and peeling paint. Getting paint to stick on crumbling concrete and masonry is like painting sand; you need to remove as much of the loose material as you can. Sandblasters rent for $30 to $40 per day, but you also need to buy silica and rent an air compressor. An air compressor with 20 psi rents for about $40 a day, and silica costs about $7 a bag (you'll probably need at least five bags). Another option is to add sand to a pressure washer to combine the cleaning action of a pressure washer and the stripping action of a sandblaster. Check with a rental store or paint store to see how to do it. This combination can be used for most coated surfaces including wood. Keep yourself well-protected if you plan to run a sandblaster, and count on a fair amount of clean-up when you're finished.

Etching new concrete is a very effective way of giving it tooth. Etching helps to condition older masonry after most of the peeling paint or crumbling masonry has been scraped out. Add muriatic acid to water, brush the solution on the dampened concrete, and work it in to the cracks with a wire or stiff brush. Muriatic acid foams as it works—anything not foaming isn't getting etched and should be recleaned. Muriatic acid burns nearly anything it contacts, so protect yourself with neoprene gloves, goggles, and a respirator. The vapors of undiluted muriatic acid will burn your lungs, and I can vouch for that. A long-handled, stiff-bristled brush is your best bet for etching walls and floors, letting you keep your distance from the caustic solution.

I use concrete caulk and caulk backing for serious repairs like this foundation crack. Make sure the caulk backing is at least ½ in. from the outer edge of the crack, or it will push the caulk out.

Repairing masonry A shop vacuum is ideal for getting all the dirt out of masonry joints and cracks before you prime and paint. I clean masonry by vacuuming up the loose mortar, then reversing the suction to blow any remaining dust out. Smaller cracks and chips of loose masonry also can be cleaned with a wire brush (be sure to wear good gloves to save your knuckles). If you're using a concrete patch, be sure to dampen the masonry first to give the patch something to stick to. Limit concrete repairs to those recommended by the manufacturer: Any larger repairs probably won't hold up, especially where concrete is exposed to freeze-thaw cycles.

Priming masonry As I mentioned in Chapter 2, latex is the primer of choice for most masonry because it can move as the masonry expands and contracts. Latex also breathes—an important consideration when coating something as porous as concrete or brick. Latex can be used as a primer on older, weathered masonry that isn't highly alkaline. Emulsabond added to latex makes a great masonry primer, although some products, such as Okon's line of concrete sealers, Loxon by Sherwin Williams, and Pittsburgh's Alkali-Resistant primers, may not need the extra sticking power.

Most reputable paint companies have block fillers, alkali-resistant primers, and surface sealers for any masonry application. The type of primer you use should be part of a paint system, to ensure compatibility with the finish coats. The primer you pick will also depend on the age and condition of the masonry. Always read the label.

PAINT FAILURE: CAUSES AND SOLUTIONS

Paint can fail for many reasons. Here are the most common problems, and ways to fix them—or avoid them altogether.

Peeling

The main cause of peeling is moisture. Peeling can happen quickly if enough water migrates through the siding, or over time as wet wood swells and later

Poor preparation and moisture were the culprits behind the blistering on this window frame. You will avoid problems like this if you prep thoroughly and make sure your painting surface is clean, dry, and dull.

contracts. It's easy to repaint, but the source of the water must be fixed for the paint to last.

As I noted in Chapter 2, a family generates a fair amount of water vapor each day. Much of the moisture is vented out, but during the colder months some of it migrates through the walls, especially in bathrooms and kitchens. Even a vapor barrier collects moisture that eventually ends up passing through the exterior walls. New construction can also generate a fair amount of moisture as the building materials cure.

Wood has to be dry for paint or stain to stick to it. Bare or new wood often contains excessive moisture from too-short curing or exposure to rain or high humidity. If exterior siding is built too close to the ground, or is exposed to leaking downspouts, water will saturate the wood and force paint off the surface.

You can prevent moisture damage by back-priming dry, new siding. Older siding can ventilate if it isn't caulked under each lap or if it's wedged open. Keeping the siding uncaulked on the horizontal laps is usually enough to allow moisture to escape. If the house has no vapor barrier, I recommend a thorough prep job and recoating with two coats of primer and two coats of latex.

Blistering

Blistering is also caused by moisture trapped under paint. The difference is that blisters happen with new paint, often with help from the sun's heat. Heat can vaporize the solvents in new paint and force water migrating through walls to vaporize under the paint, causing blisters. Blistering also can occur if a water-based coating doesn't have time to cure before being exposed to rain, dew, or fog.

You can determine the cause of blistering by looking beneath the blister. Bare wood indicates moisture as the culprit. If

This checking was missed during the initial prep. If it isn't fixed, it will eventually crack and peel.

you see another layer of paint, heat probably is to blame. In that case, you only have to prep, prime, and repaint when the siding is cooler. However, if the blistering was caused by migrating moisture, you should caulk and vent the siding to prevent moisture from getting trapped inside.

Checking and cracking

Checking shows up as small cracks in the top coat of paint. It's the first indication that the paint has lost its elasticity. Older, thicker coats of paint become brittle. Sometimes a new coat of paint will check if it is incompatible with the primer. Checking can be fixed by wire brushing or, in more severe cases, scraping and sanding down to a layer that is intact. Checking on new paint can disappear after all the coats have cured and weathered, but older coats of paint often deteriorate from checking to full-fledged cracking.

Alligatoring is usually found where exposure to sun and moisture is the highest, such as on these west-facing steps.

As the wood continues to expand and contract, checking on brittle older paint slowly widens, forming cracks. As the cracks enlarge, water enters and helps to finish off the coat of paint. You know this process has occurred when you find paint that has curled up, exposing bare wood.

Hardboard wax stains

Hardboards have been around for a while and today are quite popular as pre-painted siding. They are made from wood pulp formed under pressure. During the process, waxes are added for water resistance. However, these waxes can migrate to the surface of the hardboard, leading to paint problems.

Wax will bleed if rain or other exterior moisture gets into the wood through unsealed areas, if vaporized moisture migrates out of the house through the walls, or if dark colors on the hardboard increase the heat, especially on southern exposures.

A wax bleed is a dark discoloration that looks like mildew. Check by applying a small amount of bleach to the stain. Bleach will kill mildew on contact, but it won't affect wax.

You can remove wax with thinner, but you first need to get down to the wood. This means scraping and sanding. A good vapor barrier under the siding will prevent future wax bleed—without it, you're fighting a losing battle.

Older hardboard can be a challenge to paint. Hardboards are grainless and non-porous like vinyl or metal, but they expand and contract like wood if they absorb moisture. You can do everything by the book and still not win. Try prepping the siding (after getting down to a good layer) with an oil-based exterior primer, or even a metal primer for extra adhesion. If the hardboard can be back-primed with a thick coat of primer, then sealed with high-end latex, you should have a long-lasting coating. A lighter color will keep the surface heat lower.

The good news is that cracking doesn't indicate the need for venting or any other structural changes. Rather, cracking indicates a problem with the coats of paint. The cracked areas need to be taken down to the wood or to a layer of good paint, if any exists. Remember: You have to prime and recoat whenever you get down to bare wood. You should use latex on exteriors wherever possible. It doesn't get as brittle as oil-based paints and it lets more moisture pass through.

Alligatoring

Alligatoring is small cracked squares that resemble—you guessed it—alligator skin. This is a serious problem, indicating advanced cracking, down to bare wood. You need to act soon to protect the siding. Alligatored paint should be completely scraped and sanded down to the wood, then primed and coated with a high-end top coat. One nice thing about alligatored paint: It scrapes off quickly and easily, in a shower of paint chips. Two primer coats provide extra insurance against premature paint failure. Although this process takes longer, the increased adhesion pays off.

Stains

There are two basic types of stains: those made by metal, and wood stains such as tannin and mildew. Metal staining usually comes from uncoated gutters, downspouts, and screens, and shows up as a dark wash that fans out from the source. Nails also do their share of staining, usually on semi-clear or clear coatings. Metal stains on wood can be removed with a wood cleaning system like those mentioned on p. 99, but you also need to coat the source of the staining. Gutters and downspouts can be coated with a metal primer (see pp. 108-109). Sealing nail heads can be tedious; you need to sand each nail head and individually coat it with metal primer. You may want to do this only on the most visible areas.

Tannin staining comes from cedar and redwood, usually when the wood is new. Tannin bleeds through paint, especially latex, and leaves a reddish-brown stain. I once tried to cover up tannin stains with several coats of sprayed latex, all to no avail. I now know that cedar or redwood needs time to cure. Then it should be cleaned of any existing staining and primed with two coats of alkyd exterior primer. Stain blockers with shellac, such as Kilz, are also good for tannin stains.

Chalking

Chalking is a powdery layer on paint. The age-old test for chalking is to run your hand over a portion of siding. No chalk means the paint is still in good shape. Chalking results from the migration of the paint binders onto the wood. It's normal on older coats of paint and indicates that the paint is aging normally—also, that you should think about recoating before the paint degrades further. Chalking on newer coats of paint isn't such a good sign: It shows that the paint is too thin or has too little or too much pigment. Latex paints will chalk if they were applied when the temperature was too low.

Chalking is easy to remove. All you need is a garden hose and a stiff brush. However, you should recoat with primer before applying a top coat.

Efflorescence

Masonry has its own set of paint problems, often caused by moisture and high alkalinity. Water that enters and moves through the masonry leaches salts out to the surface, leaving a white coat that will loosen up paint.

The first thing you need to do is to find and fix the source of the moisture. If you don't, water will keep on moving through the masonry and repeating the process. Sealing the masonry will help, but only for a while. Once the moisture problem is fixed, you can wire-brush, grind with a resin wheel, or sandblast the peeling paint. If you have a scraper on the back of the wire brush, use it instead of a good scraper, since concrete will quickly dull a good tool. Sandblasting should remove all the efflorescence, but wire-brushing alone will not. If you wire-brushed, you should use muriatic acid to make sure all the efflorescence is gone.

When the surface is completely prepped, prime the masonry with a masonry surface sealer, or a masonry primer that uses Emulsabond with the top coat.

Saponification

Like most paint problems, this starts with moisture moving through the masonry. Bleeding salts cause oil-based paint to go from soft to tacky, and eventually fall or slough off. The paint should be removed and the source of the moisture fixed before priming and recoating. If the whole coat has to come off, you might be better to double-prime, then recoat with latex.

Spalling

When moisture gets into concrete through cracks or pores, freezing temperatures cause the moisture to expand the crack and eventually break off sections of concrete. Spalling, or chipping, happens closer to the surface, usually in the form of convex divots that seldom get larger than 5 in. or 6 in. (although I've seen older concrete with some pretty big spalling). Concrete that is low in cement and high in sand or lime has a much greater tendency to spall and crumble.

Spalled areas can be filled with Thoropatch. Small spalled chunks of concrete sometimes can be glued with concrete caulking: fill the hole with the caulking, replace the spalled concrete, and seal the edges.

The new coat of paint on this metal siding didn't flash in time to prevent sagging. I had to strip and repaint the entire side.

Spalling can be prevented by sealing the concrete with Okon or another masonry surface sealer from a good paint company. First, repair any cracks with a good concrete caulk and, if necessary, double-coat them.

PROBLEMS WITH NEW PAINT APPLICATIONS

When you get to the point where you're ready to prime and paint, make certain that outdoor conditions are favorable and the surfaces are completely clean and dry. You'd be surprised how many paint jobs fail because of bad weather, cold temperatures, too-thin coats, or other application problems. Many contractors have ended up working for peanuts because they rushed the job when conditions weren't ideal.

After you've painted your exterior, keep an eye on it: New paint problems will show up within 24 hours.

Sagging

Once I was painting a commercial building with metal siding and everything was on schedule—including fall weather. Hoping to beat the dropping temperatures, I sprayed a top coat on the siding, figuring that it would at least flash before the evening temperatures got too low. The next day I saw that almost all the paint had sagged, resembling curtains on the siding.

Sagging can also happen if you coat too thickly or use too much thinner. The latter is more likely to happen if you spray. High temperatures will make paint thicken, and extreme low temperatures will thin the paint and cause it to dry too slowly (that's what happened in my case). Trying to paint over a smooth, glossy surface also can make paint sag or bubble as it dries.

Crawling

If you've ever tried to paint over a waxy or greasy surface, you know what crawling is—the paint instantly shrinks to form small pools. If this happens, you should stop, clean off the paint, and clean the contaminated area with thinner. Let the thinner dry before you try to recoat.

Streaking

Streaking happens to latex paints, especially darker ones, that are exposed to rain, dew, or other forms of moisture before the paint has time to flash. (Because of their extra pigments, darker latexes take longer to dry.) Streaking looks like the new coat of paint washed off. Blisters or bubbles may even appear. If you see evidence of streaking, don't worry. When this happened to me, I feared that I would have to remove the entire coat. But the coat recovered completely after a good rinsing with a garden hose.

How to thicken and thin paint

Paint that has sat on your shelf for a long time will separate—when you open the can, you'll see the solvent on top. A good mixing will even the consistency, but if the paint is still too thin after mixing, you can do one of two things.

If the paint is oil-based, you can leave the lid off to let some of the solvent evaporate. You can't do this with latex, however, or it will form a skin. To thicken latex, you'll need to batch it with two or more gallons of the same paint (see p. 85). This technique also works for thickening oil-based paint.

Paint can get too thick if the lid wasn't airtight, or if it was stored at too-low temperatures. It's always easier to thin paint than to thicken it. Start by pouring the amount of paint that you think you'll need into another can. (That way the whole can won't be ruined if you make the paint too thin.) Add a small amount of thinner (for oil paints) or water (for latex paints) at a time, bearing in mind that a little thinner goes a long way.

Slow drying

Less-than-ideal conditions such as cool temperatures and extreme humidity slow the drying process, especially for oil-based paint. Surfaces contaminated with dirt or grease also increase the drying time, because binders in the paint can't penetrate the surface. The biggest danger with slow drying is that the paint is more likely to sag or drip on vertical surfaces. Prolonged drying also can cause the paint to wrinkle or spot-dry on flat surfaces (see p. 118).

Humidity can really slow the drying time. It's a good idea to wait for drier weather conditions. If you have to paint in questionable weather, add Japan Drier to your shopping list; it will help oil-based paint flash sooner (see p. 24).

Poor hiding

Hiding is the ability of paint to cover the coat beneath it. The better the paint and pigments, the better the hiding. Ironically, darker paint won't easily hide lighter colors. That's because hiding pigments are white, and darker colors have less of them. I once had an interior paint job that required a ceiling to be painted dark purple, and I mean dark. It took five coats of very good paint to get it dark enough. Unless you're repainting with the same color, chances are you'll need two coats—maybe more.

This paint wrinkled because the surface wasn't deglossed. Deglossers or denatured alcohol will break the gloss of a top coat. Sanding also works, but it takes more elbow grease.

I leave a hard line at the edge of my touch-ups—it actually blends better than a feathered stroke. I gave these touch-ups a second coat with a Long Reach roller; it's much faster and leaves a perfect edge and texture.

Paint that is applied too thin is the usual cause of poor hiding. Other reasons include overly thinned paint, extremely porous surfaces, uneven paint mixing, a poor-quality paint brush or roller, and extreme color changes.

Spotting

Spotting is usually an oil-based problem resulting from uneven drying. Spotting shows up as a change in the sheen and later as a color variation. The problem is caused by spreading paint too thin, or from moisture in the paint that condenses as the paint dries. Poor-quality paint also will cause paint to spot.

Wrinkling

Wrinkling resembles lizard skin. The main reason paint wrinkles is that it has been applied over a coat that isn't dry. Painting a surface that is too hot or cold also will make paint wrinkle, as will applying the paint too thickly. A new coat will wrinkle if it's applied to a surface that hasn't been properly deglossed and dulled (see p. 117). The best way to avoid wrinkling is to make sure the existing coat is thoroughly dry and dull, and that the surfaces are within the temperatures listed by the manufacturer.

Cratering

Also known as pinholing, cratering is caused by trapped air in the paint film. Lower-quality paint is more prone to cratering than paints with good leveling qualities. Paint that is too thick, surfaces that are too hot, and new, unprimed roller covers all can contribute to the problem.

Lap marks

When you paint over a coat that hasn't completely dried, the overlapped paint tears from the surface and leaves a paint strip, or lap mark. The lap mark dries darker or with a different finish. Lap marks can also result from coating the surface too thinly or painting a hot surface.

If you're painting an area that's a little on the warm side, paint smaller sections, or wait for the area to cool down. Porous surfaces can speed up the drying time, so you might want to give concrete block or porous wood a second coat of primer before applying the top coat.

Another type of lap mark, called hat-banding, happens when you cut in an area with a brush, then go back over it with a roller. Cutting in with a brush leaves a thinner coat of paint than a roller, so the cut-in area shows up as a lighter-colored band. A second coating for the cut-in area usually solves the problem. If everything isn't getting a second coat of paint, the second cut-in coat may need to be thinned to blend in. One way to avoid the problem is to cut in after you've rolled. If you're good with a roller, you'll leave only an inch to cut in, which reduces any potential hat-banding.

EXTERIOR PAINTING PROCESS

Painting the exterior is technically the same as painting the interior, but outdoor surfaces and conditions sometimes require a different approach.

Applications

The sheer size of an exterior job allows you to cover more area quickly. Whenever possible, I prefer to spray. For speed and efficiency, it can't be beat, even when you allow extra time for masking. Of the three application techniques, spraying applies the thickest coating, followed by rolling, with brushing a distant third.

Spraying Vertical spray patterns usually are preferable indoors, accentuating the height of the walls. Outdoors, however, horizontal spraying tends to work best, not only for siding, but also for surfaces with no apparent direction, such as stucco.

Even with my trusty Long Reach roller, I'll need a brush to paint the angles on this narrow soffit. I keep an angled sash brush nearby to reach hard-to-roll spots.

Regular maintenance allows the owners of this house to paint it themselves without being overwhelmed. They paint only two sides each year. Using a top-notch siding stain such as Sikkens helps

People notice front doors. An extra coat of glossy spar varnish on this older screen door brought the finish back to life. I recoated the main door with a semi-gloss spar varnish. They look great together, proving the value of paint maintenance.

Rolling If you opt not to spray, you can make short work of exterior painting with a roller that's close to the width of your siding. After spreading the paint with the roller, you can make a finishing stroke with a brush to erase stipple. However, there are times when you don't want to leave brush marks, such as when you're recoating or touching up a sprayed coat of paint. Spraying doesn't leave any texture; rolling a new coat over a sprayed coat is the ideal way to apply paint without leaving much texture.

Brushing Brushing a new coat over a sprayed coat will leave marks that won't blend well. But brushing is still the only way to cut in siding and paint trim. The technique is the same as for interiors. As with any exterior application, you should avoid brushing a dark surface that's hot to the touch.

This spray shield keeps most of the spray off the high trim and the roof. I only spray if the weather is good and the air is calm.

If I'm spraying, it might only take a day to paint all the siding on a house. Brushing out the trim is what takes time. However, the trim and other color accents are focal points on a house, so make them look their best.

Maintenance

Sometimes only parts of the house need upkeep—the deck or the south-facing windows. I've often noticed that the first thing that happens to the exterior is an accumulation of dirt and grime on the siding, windows, and doors. With enough moisture the dirty areas can give rise to mildew, or at least act as a magnet for more dirt. Exterior windows are also quick to show signs of wear. Because deep colors absorb more heat, darker trim and windows take even more of a beating.

Regular maintenance allows you to chip away at the job instead of having to paint the entire house. Maintenance greatly extends the life of any paint job, and is much less costly than waiting for all the paint to go. If you postpone recoating until the entire house needs it, your trim, windows, and doors will suffer.

Painting maintenance also allows you to keep the focal points of the house, such as the front door and the trim, looking new. Best of all, maintenance takes less preparation than a full-scale painting job.

Exterior painting sequence

To minimize touch-ups, painting from top to bottom is usually best. The eaves and soffits are the highest features on most houses—that's where you should begin. I paint the windows and doors last. Any spatter from the siding can be removed before I paint the trim. Also, windows and doors require detail work that creates less spatter.

Spray shields don't need to be fancy, just straight. Keep the spray stroke within 1 ft. of either end of the shield.

A bead of long-lasting caulk works well for sealing exterior windows and goes on faster than window putty. Keep the bead narrow and try not to smear the window.

However, you need to reconsider the top-to-bottom sequence when you're spraying. This is my sequence for exterior spraying:

1. Prep and prime the trim and windows.
2. Prep the siding to the point where it's ready to spray.
3. Mask off all the trim, windows, and anything not being sprayed the same color.
4. Spray the siding.
5. After 24 hours, remove the masking and apply the finish coats to the trim.

Prep and prime the trim first so any scraping, grinding, or sanding won't threaten the finished coats on the siding. Once the masking is off, you only need to brush the top coats on the trim.

Begin spraying the siding just below the eaves and soffits. Use a spray shield to minimize overspray until you've sprayed 1 ft. below the soffit. If you're spraying a gable, you need to use a spray shield to protect the roof from overspray. When you've finished spraying the siding, go back and brush the trim, beginning with the eaves and soffits, and work down to the windows and doors. One way to

Caulking can quickly blister your fingers. I often use a finger from a discarded rubber glove as protection.

keep a handle on overspray and paint runs is to spray first thing in the morning, after the air has warmed up and the dew has dried, but before any wind kicks up. (It also helps to check the weather to make sure conditions are optimum for painting.) Spraying in the morning also ensures that the siding or trim won't be too hot to paint. Always paint the warmer, south-facing side of the house first.

If you decide to apply the paint with a roller and then back-brush for the right texture, use the same sequence as for brushing: high to low, with the windows and doors last.

Check your work often when rolling or brushing. The key to minimizing runs is not to apply too much paint or stain with the first stroke. If you see paint starting to run during the unloading stroke, it may continue to run even after you've spread it. This is especially true when painting sharp-edged trim. There's a fine line between the right amount of paint and too much, so inspect your work regularly.

Setting a drop cloth is one of the first things I do before prepping or painting—inside or out. Drop cloths always make cleaning up easier.

Caulking

Caulking repairs cracks and seals gaps between siding and trim. It is a quick, effective solution for moisture and air problems. Before you start painting the top coats, take a close look around the windows and trim for places where moisture and air need to be kept out. All

When working outside, I make sure I have plenty of wood on hand to keep the ladders level.

Scaffolding comes in handy for larger exterior projects such as this two-story house. Most rental stores carry scaffolding equipment.

the trim around windows should be sealed, especially the top and bottom sashes. Exterior sashes suffer the most of any exterior material. Their flat angle collects moisture and sunlight, especially around basement windows.

Avoid sealing under the lap of wood siding. Moisture escaping from the interior needs to have an exit, and caulking the siding lap makes it harder for the moisture to escape. However, the joint where the siding meets the corner should be caulked to prevent rain and dew from getting in.

Masking

Exterior masking of windows, walkways, etc., is usually done only for spraying. The methods and materials used for masking are described on pp. 38-42. Note that you need to be careful about the length of time you leave the masking on, and the kind of tape you use. I recommend using a tape specifically designed for masking. Some tapes leave adhesive behind or tear the paint if left on too long. I mask shortly before spraying and remove the masking as soon as the paint has cured, usually the next morning. Remove the tape slowly. If you pull it off too fast, the paint may rip.

I use a drop cloth whenever I'm brushing or rolling. Get into the habit of keeping a drop cloth under your work site, whether you're scraping, sanding, or painting. Think of the cloth as a security blanket for easier clean-up.

Ladders and scaffolding

When you're painting outdoors, the style of ladder and scaffolding is less important than the sturdiness of the equipment. Older equipment that leaves you swaying in the breeze can be distracting, to say the least. If you plan to rent the equipment, get an extension ladder that's longer than you think you need. A ladder that isn't extended all the way provides double rungs for easier footing.

Be careful not to lean a bare ladder end against the siding or eaves; once you begin moving around, the ladder end will mar the finish. Another thing—stay sharp when you're working above ground. It's those short lapses in concentration that lead to accidents. Take a break when you find your attention fading or your legs tiring.

You need to scrub a deck for best results. I use a car-washing brush with an extension pole. Although some cleaners can be applied with a garden sprayer, decks benefit from a more strenuous cleaning. Heavy concentrations of dirt and weathering may require more than one washing.

Decks

Coating a deck can be a simple, straightforward procedure requiring one day for washing the wood, one day for drying, and a third to apply the coating. But you may need to budget more time for prep if your deck is in rough shape.

Choosing a coating The rule of thumb is to recoat with the existing coating—oil over oil, semi-transparent over the same, etc. However, if your deck requires much prep and repriming (for a solid stain, for instance), feel free to use a different primer and top coat than the original. A new deck, of course, offers unlimited opportunities.

Don't forget to consider maintenance when choosing a deck coating. Ideally, you should choose a coating that will last a long time and give you the fewest headaches. My idea of a maintenance headache is having to strip, prep, and recoat every year or two. A deck that is washed and/or recoated yearly should last 10 years without needing total stripping and recoating. Not every deck needs to be recoated yearly, but if you're going to the trouble of washing it, you might as well give it a thin maintenance coat; deck cleaners strip some of the coating. A contractor I know says maintaining your deck is like keeping the oil in your car clean—you can pay a little now or pay a lot later.

I use a car-washing brush to coat decks quickly. First I cut in the edges and railing with a paint brush. It was getting warm when I did this job, so I cut in shorter sections to avoid lap marks.

There's a full range of finishes for decks, from clear coats to paint. Clear coats are often used to show off a cedar or redwood deck, but they have less UV protection and require a bit more maintenance in the form of washings, recoating, sealers, and UV protectors. All those coatings add up to what is called a higher build, or thick coating.

UV protection increases with semi-transparents and trans-oxides. Most contractors prefer these stains for decks. A semi-transparent stain can provide color and give you a penetrating, long-lasting coating that requires comparatively little maintenance.

Solid stains, especially oil-based stains, tend to peel more, although I've been able to increase the sticking power of oil stains by adding Penetrol (see p. 24). If you're leaning towards a solid deck stain, I recommend trying a durable high-end acrylic, which is less likely to peel, if the right primer is used.

Cleaning and prepping decks Before you apply any coating, you need to inspect your deck. You'll probably find a few boards that have worked loose and need to be retightened. Better decks are screwed together; nailed-on decking eventually works loose. Use the same wood to replace any boards, especially if you're coating with a clear or semi-transparent stain. You'll need to scrape and sand any badly peeling areas.

Cleaning the deck is the most important part of preparation—most decks don't need more than a good washing. Rinse the deck and the surrounding vegetation before and after you wash the deck. Even biodegradable wood cleaners are strong enough to burn vegetation.

I'm back-priming this redwood with a clear coat to ensure a long-lasting seal. Although a 4-in. China bristle brush works well, a sprayer and back-rolling system would be faster for back-priming an entire deck.

New deck wood should be cleaned before a coating is applied, but some wood cleaners should not be used on redwood or cedar. Again, read the labels carefully.

Decks with hot tubs and pools will often have black stains. Chemicals pool on the deck and eat away protective coatings, leaving the surface open to mildew, dirt, and weathering. The bleach solution described on p. 100 makes a decent mildew cleaner. Deck cleaners also do a very good job of removing mildew and black stains.

Coating the deck After washing the deck, it's important to let all the moisture evaporate. Wait at least 24 hours before coating—it doesn't hurt to wait even longer to make sure the deck is completely dry. Hurrying the drying time only weakens the finished product, so be patient.

You'll only need to prime the deck if you plan to coat it with paint. Stains, whether solid, semi-transparent, or clear, don't need priming. Back-priming is recommended to preserve any exterior wood.

6

COMING CLEAN

The best method for minimizing overspray and runs is to check the area you've just sprayed. Checking is especially important when you're spraying borders, spraying in a breeze, or spraying latex, which sets up quickly.

Just as preparation means every process leading up to the actual painting, clean-up involves much more than rinsing your roller cover and washing your hands. Thorough cleaning is critical if you want your painting tools to last. Also, community regulations regarding paint and solvents have grown more stringent. You need to learn techniques for safe disposal of these hazardous products.

However, your first step in cleaning up should be checking the areas you've just painted, so you can correct overspray and runs.

SURFACE CLEAN-UP

A damp rag is best for cleaning up latex overspray, or a thinner-dampened rag if you're spraying oil-based paint. The key is to clean up before the paint flashes and dries—dried runs and overspray can be a real challenge to remove. Overspray is tough to remove completely. I usually just recoat the oversprayed area with the original paint.

On some surfaces, overspray can't always be painted over. Shingles have to be attended to quickly, and if they are at all hot, the paint will set up instantly. Your options for cleaning shingles are limited. You can try scrubbing the area with a strong detergent or thinner before the paint sets up (all the more

Resin-wheel brushes are ideal for feathering paint on concrete and for removing paint from all kinds of surfaces, including metal and wood. Resin keeps the brush from clogging up; paint can't stick to it.

reason to be extra careful and mask first). If I spot overspray on concrete, I'll take a damp rag and, if necessary, a wire brush to correct the problem as soon as possible. Thicker overspray or spilled paint that has dried requires a resin-wheel brush attached to a drill.

Use a dampened brush or rag to feather out a run that's still wet. Lightly dampen the brush in a solvent and dab the run with the tip of the brush. Once a run has begun to harden, wait for it to dry completely, then use a sharp 5-in-1 to slice the run off. After removing a dried run, lightly sand around the edges to feather the outline. Carefully recoat using the dabbing method.

A 5-in-1 wrapped in a clean rag is great for touching up precisely and leaving a clean line.

TOOLS AND TECHNIQUES FOR CLEAN-UP

You probably already have most of the tools and materials needed to clean paint brushes and roller covers. Here's a quick run-down.

Tools

You'll need a 5-in-1 scraper, a wire brush, and two 5-gallon buckets—one for water and another for thinner. Save a few empty paint cans for storing new and used thinner, and don't forget to label every can or bucket as you use it: Unlabeled cans quickly turn into frustrating mystery cans. Rounding out the necessary cleaning tools are a hose nozzle, a brush comb, and a roller and brush spinner. The spinner is the fastest way to clean brushes and roller covers, but a wire brush and brush comb also work well.

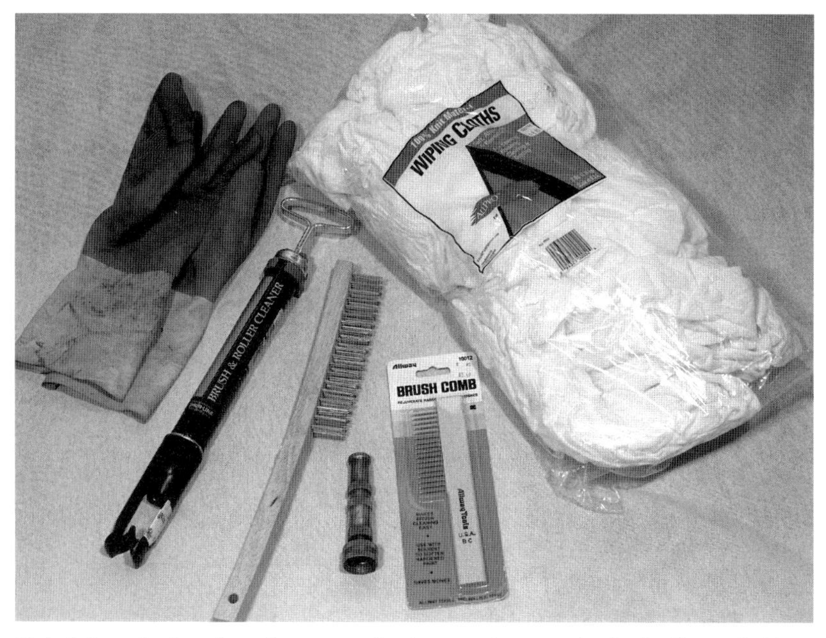

Helpful tools for cleaning up painting equipment include (from left) rubber gloves, a brush and roller spinner, a wire brush, a brass hose nozzle, a paint brush comb, and clean rags.

Solvents

Soap and water is the recommended solvent any time you're cleaning up latex coatings. For day-to-day cleaning, I just use water, rinsing tools, brushes, and roller covers, rinsing until the water runs clear. At the end of a job (or work week), I clean brushes and rollers more thoroughly, using soap and water. Water-borne stains take a little more work: I wash the applicator with soap and water, then with thinner, then once more with soap and water. Latex additives such as Emulsabond are extremely sticky, and clean-up requires the same three-part system used for water-borne products.

Thinner is the standard solvent for oil-based coatings. The more refined the thinner, the better it cleans. I recommend using a thinner made by one of the paint manufacturers. Duosol by Pratt & Lambert and Leptyne by Pittsburgh Paints are two very good thinners, and there are lots of others. There is an odorless version of Leptyne thinner that has lower VOCs. Never use lacquer thinner as a cleaning solvent—it is extremely sticky when it dries.

A word of caution: With flash points that range from 80°F to 125°F, thinners can spontaneously ignite. Check the flash point of the thinner you're using and be very careful about storing it. Thinners mixed with certain coatings, such as spar varnish (flash point of 74°F) or sanding sealer (flash point of 68°F), are very dangerous if stored near or in heat. I try to store highly volatile coatings and thinners in the coolest part of a building, and always keep a fire extinguisher nearby.

Even thinner-soaked rags can cause a fire if the vapors and heat are concentrated enough. Vapors from solvents build up fast in a closed container. Solvent-soaked rags should be left out to dry and never kept in a sealed container.

If you just need short-term storage, a stirring stick is ideal for suspending brushes in solvent. Fill a paint can with enough solvent to cover the brush bristles. Fasten the brush to the stick with a rubber band, keeping its bristles off the bottom of the can.

Spin a brush or roller cover inside a bucket or garbage can to avoid spattering diluted paint. If any paint sticks to the brush filaments, clean it off with a wire brush, then rinse and spin again.

Techniques

If you've invested good money in quality painting equipment, you want it to last as long as possible. Solid clean-up is the key.

Cleaning brushes Good brushes start at $10, and a good brush will serve you a long time if you clean and store it right. I use two methods for cleaning and storing brushes and roller covers—one for day-to-day use, the other for the end of the job. The day-to-day type of cleaning is faster, as the brushes don't always have to be completely cleaned and dried. When I take a break or stop for the day, I rinse the brush in the proper solvent (water or thinner) and either hand-spin it or use a spinner to remove most of the paint. I spin the brush briefly, wire-brush it, then store it in solvent. I use a stirring stick to suspend the brush in the solvent because if a brush is left sitting on its bristles for long, the taper will be damaged. A rubber band around the handle of the brush puts the weight on the stirring stick.

For a thorough cleaning, I use a brush and roller spinner. I rinse the brush, insert the handle into the spinner, hold the spinner and brush in a 5-gallon bucket or garbage can, and pump the spinner to remove the paint. I repeat this as many as five times before the brush is totally clean. When using thinner, I soak

Paint builds up at the base of the brush. When clogged paint forces the bristles apart, the brush becomes a "club" that isn't good for much more than priming and dusting.

the brush, drain the excess, and spin it. I pour the used thinner into a bucket of dirty thinner.

A wire brush or brush comb also cleans brushes, it just takes longer. If all I have on hand is a wire brush, I soak the paint brush, wire-brush it, and then hand-spin it. To test the brush, I squeeze the bristles to see if the solvent comes out clean.

Storing brushes At the end of a job or work week, I give my brushes a good cleaning with a brush spinner. After spinning the brush clean—and while it's still damp—I coat the bristles with a bar of soap. This helps preserve the original shape and taper of the brush, which is critical for painting a smooth, clean edge. You may have noticed that, just like hair, bristles that get completely dried out have an electrical charge and tend to stick out. A coating of soap helps to "block" the bristles with a washable coating.

Storing the brush in a container is necessary to maintain its shape. Brushes that aren't kept in some type of shaper will dry with their filaments going in all directions—and trying to get stray filaments to behave is like trying to control a cowlick. Better brushes come in wrappers that hold the shape of the filaments and taper, but over time the wrappers themselves lose shape. When a wrapper gets old, you can make new inserts to strengthen it. Simply cut the insert out of thin cardboard, shape it around the brush, and seal it with a rubber band. Although the original wrapper is best for blocking the brush, you don't have to use it. Even a paper towel wrapped around the brush and secured with a rubber band will keep the bristles in place.

I keep my brushes stored upside down in a tool bucket, but you can also suspend brushes from a hook. Any storage method is fine as long as you keep the brushes wrapped with the weight off the bristles.

Cleaning roller covers If I plan to use a roller cover throughout a job, I wait until the project is finished before cleaning it. For temporary storage, I keep the roller cover coated with paint and suspended from the grill in a 5-gallon paint bucket. I seal the top of the bucket with the lid, leaving the roller handle sticking out, and carefully wrap the handle with a damp rag to keep air out. The next day the roller cover is fresh and ready to go.

Roller covers hold an amazing amount of paint, even when it looks like most of the paint has been pressed out. I used to roll the excess paint on to a piece of scrap, but that wastes paint. Scraping paint out of the cover with a 5-in-1 saves material and time. You can also use a piece of cardboard curved in the shape of a roller cover to squeeze out the paint.

Washing paint out of a roller cover takes forever if you don't first squeeze out the excess. A 5-in-1 is ideal for this, or you can fashion a scraper out of cardboard. Be sure to wear rubber gloves.

Once you've removed most of the excess paint, insert the end of roller cover over the spinner, soak it with water (or thinner) and spin. Even with most of the paint scraped out, you'll find that it takes several rinse-and-spin cycles to get all the paint out of the cover.

Before I began using a spinner, I spun the roller under a hose. This also works fairly well. With the roller cover still attached to the handle, suspend the cover over a garbage can and rinse it with the hose nozzle. A roller that isn't gummed up will spin fast enough to get the paint out. Check to make sure that the ends and the inside of the cover are clean, too. Paint that hardens on the ends will ruin a roller cover.

Depending on how much it's being used, a high-end roller cover can last several jobs. I store my roller covers, most of which are 1-in. lambswool covers, in a vertical position to keep the nap intact.

Cleaning sprayers Cleaning a sprayer is a little more involved than cleaning brushes or rollers, but takes about the same amount of time. Most homeowners will opt to rent a sprayer. If you rent from a paint store, you'll probably get a checklist with the sprayer. (Even though I own a sprayer, I still refer to my own checklist when cleaning, because I know how easy it is to miss a critical step.) The sequence for cleaning sprayers is to clean the spray line, then the sprayer, gun, and spray tips.

I clean the coating out of the spray line as soon as I'm finished spraying. Here I'm pumping the coating out of the line with thinner.

To clean the spray line, set the intake tube into a 1-gallon bucket of water or thinner, depending on the type of paint or stain used. Water or thinner is necessary to push the coating out of the line. Turn the pressure all the way down, remove the tip, and aim the gun into the original can or bucket of paint. The object is to clean the coating out of the line without diluting it with water or thinner. Paint or stain travels 1 ft. per second through the line. You need to know the length of the line so you can count how long to empty it out.

After removing most of the coating from the spray line, begin pumping either water or dirty thinner (depending on the sprayed coating) through the line to begin cleaning the line and spray gun. Aim the gun into the dirty-solvent bucket and finish pumping the solvent through the line. Stop when you see the coating change to clear water or thinner. You know that the line is clean when the solvent comes out clear.

If you used thinner to clean oil-based paint out of the hose and spray gun, you're finished cleaning. Cleaning latex out of a sprayer takes a little longer. You'll need two to three buckets to get all the latex pumped out of the hose—this is critical. If left overnight, the latex will clog the line and the spray gun. Water alone won't get all the paint out. Thinner will remove any remaining latex; use one of the buckets for pumping thinner through the spray line. You also can use a product called Liquid Shield, which is non-toxic and gray water safe (see p. 99). (I always prefer using a painting product that is water-based, especially if it does the trick.)

The next step is cleaning the spray gun. If you rented the sprayer, chances are you won't have to take the gun apart and clean it; the paint or rental store will probably prefer to do it. If you do need to clean the gun, make certain that the pump is off and all the pressure is out of the line. Remove the gun from the line using two wrenches, taking care not to strip the brass fittings. Inside the gun handle you'll find a filter that also needs cleaning. The inside of the spray line should be coated with thinner, so I clean the filter with thinner and a toothbrush. The tip will need cleaning, too. I use a stiff toothbrush—nothing that will scratch and ruin the expensive tip. Finally, you need to roll up the spray line and tie it off.

Be careful not to damage the sprayer tip. One small scratch causes spitting and uneven spray patterns. Too much pressure with a wrench scratched this tip.

Cleaning yourself You can minimize the paint that gets on your clothes, skin, and hair if you wear a lightweight painting suit and a spray hood for protection against spray mist. Still, it's easy to get lax with things like painting coveralls and hoods, especially when it's hot outside.

Latex coatings are the easiest to remove. Usually soap and warm water will get most of the paint off your skin. It takes repeated shampooing to get latex out of hair—denatured alcohol gets the paint out fast, but it isn't great for hair. Only use it when you can follow up with a mild cleanser or shampoo.

It really pays to cover up when you're painting with solvent-based coatings. If you don't, you'll need thinner to remove dried paint from your skin and hair. You don't have to use thinner if the paint on your skin or hair is still damp. INZ is a non-toxic, biodegradable cleaner that works great for cleaning solvent and paint off anything, including skin (as well as brushes and roller covers). INZ must be combined with soap and water to work, but it definitely beats washing yourself with thinner. Thinner is very toxic and absorbed quickly by the skin and hair. Unfortunately, there are no alternatives for cleaning dried solvent-based paints off your skin. Make sure to wash off the thinner as soon as it has taken the paint off your skin.

If you have to wash with thinner, use a straight thinner that contains no turpentine or lacquer.

DISPOSING OF PAINTS AND SOLVENTS

Paint, stain, and solvent disposal has been getting more and more attention, and rightly so—it is very important. Toxic spills don't only happen in far-off places, they happen every time leftover paint and solvents are dumped down the drain or carelessly thrown away.

Safe paint disposal

Occasionally you may come across the odd can of paint that's unusable and has to be thrown away. If there aren't any collection programs in your area, you can neutralize and dispose of the leftover coating yourself.

You'll need industrial-strength gloves, rags, cardboard scrapers, a power drill and mixing attachment (any suitable hand-mixing tool will work), 5-gallon buckets, and some ready-mix concrete, or gravel and Portland cement. Important: Before you start mixing, cover the area you're working in with plywood, cardboard, or plastic sheeting.

I use three 5-gallon buckets for mixing paint and solvent waste with concrete.

LATEX

Cans of latex paint only partly full can be solidified by evaporation. If you have more than one-third of a gallon, you should mix the latex with an absorbent material. Cat litter is recommended by most environmental agencies, but I usually mix unusable latex with Portland cement or a concrete mix. These set up much faster and cost about the same. Once the latex mixture has dried, it's ready for disposal in a landfill.

Some latex can be salvaged. Older paint that's been well-sealed and not frozen may separate over time, and the solids will feel doughy, but the paint can be revived by persistent stirring and straining. Frozen latex looks like cottage cheese. It's ruined—don't attempt to stir or strain it.

OIL-BASED OR ALKYD COATINGS

It's very important that you neutralize solvent-based coatings before disposing of them. I pour the leftover paint into a 5-gallon bucket, using cardboard to scrape all the paint from the bottom of the can. Then I add Portland cement and begin mixing with a drill attachment (mixing can be done manually, but it takes longer). I mix in gravel with a shovel for ex-

Household hazardous waste (HHW) is any home-generated product that is corrosive, combustible, toxic, or explosive, posing a threat to human health or the environment. Examples include batteries, oven cleaners, drain openers, paints and stains, paint strippers, thinners, and other solvents.

How can you tell if a coating or solvent is toxic? Read the labels, which have to state whether the product is toxic. If your product is hazardous, you need to find out the best way to store or discard it. Don't panic—even if there isn't a HHW collection program where you live, there are still plenty of quick, low-cost options for storing, disposing of, and recycling paints and solvents.

The used thinner in this container has settled, so I'm pouring off the top for reuse. I add the material at the bottom to the oil-based paint waste, which will be mixed with cement.

To neutralize paint waste, pour cement and gravel, or ready-mix concrete, into the used-paint container and mix thoroughly with a drill attachment or shovel. This inert mixture is suitable for disposal in a landfill when it has dried.

tra thickening, then seal the bucket. The mixture is now suitable for landfill disposal.

I usually wait to neutralize solvent-based paint until I have enough to make setting-up worthwhile. By then I have a fair amount of used thinner to recycle too. After each job, I pour dirty thinner into a 5-gallon container and let it settle. The waste forms a mass at the bottom that I will add to the solvent-based paints being mixed for disposal. When the waste has settled, I pour the cleared thinner into another labeled container. The recycled thinner can be used to soak brushes and roller covers. However, I won't add it to paint that will be sprayed; the thinner hasn't been filtered and has lost much of its strength.

Disposal regulations

I don't intend to lead you through all the regulations for HHW waste and disposal. Here's a brief synopsis:

Both state and federal laws hold homeowners responsible for hazardous household wastes. The laws are a bit confusing, but it helps to know that different types of wastes are regulated by different government agencies. Landfill regulations, waste-water regulations, and disposal regulations all have a say in the disposal of HHWs.

To learn more about HHW disposal on the local level, call your county department of environmental health, city landfill, or city maintenance shops. The fire department is also knowledgeable about the dangers of storing coatings such as thinner and lacquer. Colleges and universities often have extension offices with lots of information about hazardous waste. State departments of environmental quality can provide disposal guidelines and regulations for all forms of HHW—not just paints and solvents.

Every year thousands of tons of household hazardous waste end up in landfills and incinerators, or, worse, dumped down the drain. None of those destinations is designed to cope with toxic waste. Michael P. Vogel, solid waste education coordinator at Montana State University Extension Service, has written a pamphlet of HHW disposal guidelines, titled *Household Hazardous Waste-Disposal Recommendations*. You can order this free pamphlet by contacting M.S.U. Extension Service, Bozeman, MT, 59717.

These are some of Vogel's suggestions:

- Be aware of the uses and dangers of toxic products; follow directions.
- Keep unused products in the original container for safety and future reference.
- Recycle empty containers or wrap them in several layers of newspaper.
- Keep all HHW out of reach of children and pets.
- Call your state environmental office for information on HHW disposal.
- Don't bury leftover chemicals or containers in your yard or garden.
- Don't dispose of liquid chemicals with household garbage.
- Don't reuse toxic containers.
- Don't mix wastes together.

Alternatives to waste disposal

Here are my own suggestions for reducing the waste:

Consider buying less-hazardous products. Many oil-based paints and stains can be substituted with a water-soluble latex coating. As I've mentioned throughout this book, you also can buy water-borne stains and sealers that clean up with a minimum of thinner. Some homeowners are even using milk-based paints that have no toxic ingredients at all (see p. 21). Companies that manufacture milk-based paint are listed in Resources (see p. 144). Peel-Away is a very good alternative to toxic paint strippers (see pp. 109-110).

Buy only what you need, and use it up. Starting with the right amount of paint automatically minimizes the disposal problem. If you do have paint or stain left after a paint job, take care to preserve it for future use.

When I have extra paint or stain, I make sure the lid is airtight, then store the can upside down. This creates a seal that keeps air from getting inside the can. Clean the groove of the lid and firmly seal the lid with a hammer. If you find a small amount of rust in a can that's been stored, it's not a problem. Simply pour the coating into another can and, if necessary, strain it through a filter to remove any rust.

Don't store thinner or solvents upside down. They have no solids to create a seal, and solvents will leak out if the lid isn't perfectly secured.

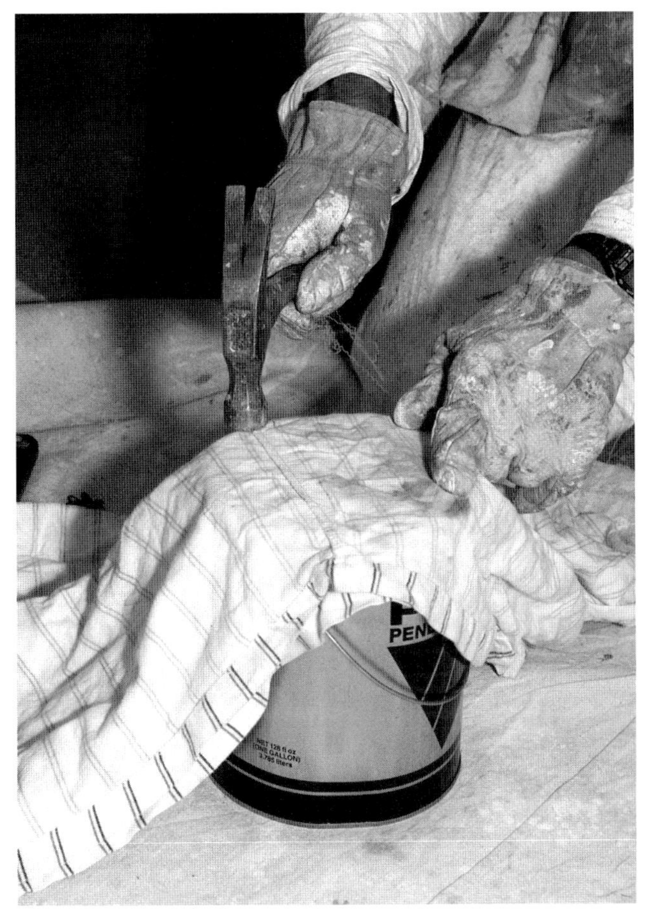

To seal a can tightly, you need to get all the paint out of the lid groove. Wipe out excess paint with a 5-in-1 scraper or drain it by punching small holes in the groove. Cover the top of the can with a rag before you hammer on the lid, to keep any remaining paint from flying.

Some paint stores offer "mis-mixes": perfectly good paint and stain sold for a fraction of the original cost. If you can find the color you're looking for, you can save a lot of money buying paint this way or at a paint swap.

Recycle or donate leftover paint. Some communities sponsor annual HHW collection days. The state environmental office should know the closest collection site in your area. Local organizations such as churches, theater groups, and civic organizations may need paint. Some landfills have ongoing summer "drop and swap" programs where people leave useable coatings at a collection area, and anyone who wants them can pick them up. Programs like this work well because they're so simple to run—nobody is left with thousands of pounds of hazardous waste.

APPENDIX

ESTIMATING SURFACE AREA

Circle: square of the radius x 3.1416 (π)
Cylinder: length x circumference + area of both ends
Trapezoid: height x ½ total length of parallel sides
Triangle (gable): base x ½ height
Walls, ceilings, and doors: length x width
Window, door, and base trim: length + width
(Contractor method for estimating interior job size: rooms with 8-ft. ceilings: total sq. ft. x 3.5; rooms with 10-ft. ceilings: total sq. ft. x 3.75)

ESTIMATING TIME

Double-hung window: three hours
Fixed window: 90 minutes
Flat doors: 90 minutes
Four- or six-panel door: three hours
A room that is 12 ft. by 14 ft. by 8 ft., with two windows and two doors, will take about 16 hours to paint, if the existing coating is in good shape. Older houses with double-hung windows, doors with raised panels, and extensive trim such as crown molding can add 50% more time to the paint job. Cracked plaster walls and ceilings also add to the time.

ESTIMATING HOW MUCH PAINT TO BUY

Estimate the area to be painted. Check the recommended coverage on the paint label, and subtract 10%: If the label recommends 400 sq. ft., plan on 360 sq. ft. Say you're painting a room that's 12 ft. by 14 ft., or 168 sq. ft. You'll need 336 sq. ft. of coverage for two top coats. That can of paint will cover your room and leave some extra for touch-ups.

GLOSSARY

Acrylic A synthetic resin used as a binder in latex coatings.
Additives Ingredients added to paint to improve flow, adhesion, drying, and resistance to mildew and insects.
Adhesion A coating's ability to stick to surfaces, usually determined by preparation and the primer coat.
Airless sprayer A type of sprayer that uses high fluid pressure to atomize the coating.
Alkyd A synthetic resin made from alcohol and acid, used in oil-based paints to increase hardness. The term is often used for oil-based primers.
Alligatoring A form of paint failure where the coating develops small patchwork cracks that extend as far as the substrate.
Applicators Tools such as brushes, rollers, sprayers, mitts, and flat pads, used to apply a coating to a surface.
Back-brushing Brushing out a rolled or sprayed coating to eliminate runs or roller stipple.
Back-priming Completely coating interior or exterior wood with primer/sealer to provide greater moisture resistance. Also, touching up with primer to make sure all surfaces are primed.
Back-rolling Rolling a sprayed coating to ensure adequate penetration and a uniform stipple. Mostly used over porous surfaces such as drywall.
Banding A spraying technique of "cutting in" around the edges of a surface, used to minimize overspray (see also Cutting in).
Binders Natural and synthetic resins in paint that bind as the paint dries, creating a film.
Bleeding Staining caused by chemical migration to the coating surface, or by the undercoat seeping through to the top coat.
Blistering A form of paint failure that occurs when large bubbles form under a coating and lift it off the surface. Caused by surface moisture or excessive surface heat.
Body The thickness of a liquid coating (see also Build).
Boxing The technique of mixing multiple containers of a coating to assure consistency of color and sheen.
Breathe A dried coating's ability to allow the passage of moisture without peeling or blistering.
Bristles The hairs or synthetic filaments of a brush, which hold and spread the coating.
Brushability A coating's ability to flow over a surface.
Brush-out A small sample of paint that's applied to a surface to determine its exact color and sheen.
Bubbles Air bubbles that vary in size from pinholes to "fish eyes," caused by foam in the coating.
Build The thickness of a dried coating, also called dry mil thickness.
Caulk A sealing material that is applied to joints with a caulk gun.
Chalking A powdery top layer on paint, indicating that the paint is slowly aging and breaking down.
Checking A minor form of paint failure that shows up as hairline cracks in the top coat.
Clear coat A transparent top coat usually applied for protection.
Coating A solvent-based or water-based layer of finish that can be protective or decorative. Includes paint, stain, varnish, lacquer, and polyurethane.
Colorant Pigment added to paints or stains for a specific color.
Coverage The area that paint will cover, expressed in sq. ft. per gallon.
Cracking Advanced checking that precedes peeling.
Crawling An application failure that causes the paint to bind to itself in globs.
Curing The final stage of drying, when a coating reaches its maximum hardness. Also used to describe the hardness of masonry.
Cutting in Brushing the edges where two surfaces meet, most often walls and ceilings and around woodwork. Can be done before or after rolling (see also Banding).
Dew point The temperature at which moisture condenses on a surface. Surface temperatures should remain at least 5 degrees above the dew point for coatings to adhere.
Drier An additive used to speed up a coating's drying time.
Drop cloth Fabric or plastic used to protect floors, carpets, and furniture.
Dryness A quality defined by stages: dust-free, tack-free, dry to the touch, dry to sand, and dry to recoat. Can be affected by temperature and humidity.
Drywall A standard interior construction material with a porous, thick paper surface.
Durability A coating's toughness, determined by its proportion of binders to pigments.
Eggshell A finish with a very slight gloss, providing greater durability than flat sheen.
Enamel A hard-finish paint that comes in several sheens, from flat to high gloss.
Epoxy A clear finish with high durability, used for some floor coatings.
Extender Inert material added to lower-quality coatings to increase volume.

Feathering In sanding, a technique for smoothing sanded edges. In brushing, a light finishing stroke used to blend wet edges.
Ferrule The metal band on a paint brush that connects the handle to the filaments.
Finish coat The top coat or finish.
5-in-1 A versatile painting tool and scraper that can be used to open lids and clean off excess paint.
Flash point The temperature at which a coating will ignite.
Flashing The first stage in the drying process, indicating that a coating has set. Also called setting up.
Flat A finish with the dullest sheen.
Flexibility A coating's ability to adhere despite temperature fluctuations.
Flow A paint's ability to spread and level smoothly.
Fungicide An additive that prevents mildew. Also called mildewcide.
Gloss A reflective paint sheen. The higher the gloss, the greater the washability and moisture resistance.
Grain, raised Swollen grain that shows up as short surface fibers, resulting from the absorption of moisture or paint solvents.
Hardboard A dense wood composite often used for exterior siding. It must be thoroughly prepped for paint to adhere well.
Hat-banding Paint overlap that dries to a darker or different color. Usually caused by uneven coating and found on cut-in areas around a room's perimeter.
Hiding A paint's ability to cover the underlying coat.
Holidays Missed or lightly painted areas on a surface.
Household hazardous waste (HHW) Paint products, cleaners, solvents, and other substances that pose environmental risks if not properly disposed of.
HVLP (high volume, low pressure) sprayer A sprayer that uses very low air pressure, creating little overspray and paint waste.
Joint compound A thick, light-colored acrylic paste used for sealing drywall and nail depressions. Also called "mud."
Lacquer A hard, quick-drying coating that dries by solvent evaporation. Most often used over a wood stain. Can be brushed or sprayed.
Lap marks Paint that appears torn, darker, or a different color. Caused by recoating before an undercoat has dried or by the coating setting up be-fore the paint strokes can be blended.
Latex A synthetic, fast-drying, water-based paint or stain. Low in odor and volatile organic compounds (see also Volatile organic compound).
LBP Lead-based paint, phased out of architectural coatings since 1971, but still present in most older homes.
Leveling A coating's ability to flatten out as it dries, hiding application marks.
Lifting The softening of a dried coat by a new coat, resulting in wrinkling.
Linseed oil The binder in oil-based coatings. One of the oldest paint ingredients.
Masking The protective covering of features that won't be painted, such as windows and flooring, using masking tape, plastic, masking paper, and drop cloths.
Masking tape Adhesive tape used to secure masking material. Comes in varying degrees of stickiness, depending on the strength and duration required.
Mildewcide A paint additive that inhibits mildew growth.
Milk paint A non-toxic paint that uses casein binder for a hard finish. One of the oldest coatings known.
Mil 1/1000 in. Used to measure a coating's thickness.
Mineral spirits A petroleum-derived solvent used in oil-based coatings such as thinner, naphtha, and turpentine.
MSDS Material Safety Data Sheet, which fully describes a coating product, including hazardous ingredients, first aid, and flammability. Can be obtained through a paint dealer or manufacturer.
Nail rusting Interior rusting caused by painting over damp nail filler.
Nap The pile thickness of roller fabric.
Oil-based Refers to slow-drying paints that use a drying oil such as linseed, and thinner for the solvent. Also known as solvent-based or alkyd paint.
Orange peel A dimpled texture in rolled or sprayed paint, caused by poor leveling.
Overspray Wasted coating lost during the spraying process.
Paint chip A paint color sample available at paint stores. Also called a swatch.
Paint conditioner An additive designed to reduce paint thickness and drying time.
Paint remover A caustic compound that softens and loosens existing layers of paint or clear coatings.
Peeling A form of paint failure indicated by the separation of the coating from the substrate.
pH The measurement of alkalinity and acidity, used to gauge whether masonry is ready to paint.
Pigments Ingredients in a coating that provide color and hiding ability.
Pinholing Surface holes in a coating, created by air bubbles.
Polyurethane A clear protective coating often applied over stains or bare wood, available in oil-based or waterborne solvents.
Polyvinyl acetate (PVA) Synthetic resin (binder) in latex coatings. Higher levels of PVA make latex tougher and less porous.
Primer A critical undercoating that seals the surface and binds the top coat to the surface. Primer has more solvent and resins and less body than top coats.
psi Pounds per square inch. Used to measure sprayer pressure.

Putty Filler material, sometimes pigmented, used to fill nail holes and wood cracks. Also used for setting glass.

Resin A natural or synthetic material that binds a coating as it dries.

Respirator A breathing device for purifying air. The most common varieties are particulate respirators and chemical respirators. The latter protect against both particulate and vapors, and are color-coded for specific use.

Roller cover A natural or synthetic fabric-coated cylinder used to apply paint or stain.

Runs Drips on a new coating caused by too thick of an application or poor adhesion.

Rust inhibitor An agent in primer that seals metal and prevents oxidation.

Sags Excessive runs in a newly applied coating.

Satin A finish with a slight degree of gloss.

Sealer A protective liquid designed to penetrate and coat a surface uniformly.

Semi-gloss A reflective sheen, one degree glossier than satin.

Semi-transparent A lightly pigmented stain with more body than a clear coating but less body than a solid stain.

Setting up A coating's first stage of drying. Also called flashing.

Sheen The degree of reflectance, or luster, in a coating, indicated as flat, eggshell, satin, semi-gloss, gloss, and high-gloss.

Shellac An all-purpose sealer and finish with a high resin content. Either used by itself or added to certain lacquers, primers, and sealers.

Skin A rubbery coating found in poorly sealed cans of paint.

Solids The coating film left after the vehicle has dried. Also, non-volatile coating compounds.

Solvent The vehicle that makes up the coating solution and evaporates as the coating dries. Can be water, alcohol, or thinners.

Spackle A lightweight, porous, easily sanded material used to fill drywall holes and cracks. Low-shrinking spackle is best.

Spatter Small drops of a coating that fall or eject from the applicator during the coating process. Thin coatings such as stain spatter the most; high-quality paints spatter least.

Spot-priming The technique of priming only bare, sanded, or stain-damaged areas of a surface.

Spotting Uneven color and sheen caused by applying a coating too thinly or too close to the dew point, or by using poor-quality paint.

Spraying An application method using compressed air or fluid to atomize the coating.

Staining Coloring a wood surface with a suspended colorant in a penetrating solvent.

Stipple A dappled paint texture left by a roller or sprayer. More pronounced when the paint is wet.

Stripping The process of removing multiple layers of coatings with paint remover.

Substrate The surface that is the base for the coating.

Surfactant Chemical soaps in latex paint that wet the surface and allow the paint to stick.

Tack cloth An oil-coated cloth used to remove dust from a surface before coating.

Tacky The stage in the drying process when dust will not stick to the coating.

Technical data Descriptive information about a coating and its use. Available at most paint stores.

Thinner A petroleum-based solvent used in oil-based coatings.

Tint base The foundation paint for colorants used in a paint system.

Toner A type of sealer applied to porous woods before staining to promote even staining over knots and other surface irregularities.

Tooth The "bite" of a surface, necessary for coatings to stick. Often created by sanding.

Touching up Can refer to recoating, covering missed areas of a new coating, or repairing an older coating.

Tung oil A very strong binder used as a wood sealant. Derived from the tung tree, this is one of the oldest known resins.

Turpentine A type of thinner used in some oil-based coatings.

Undercoat Any coat beneath the top coat.

Varnish A clear sealer that dries to a hard finish.

Vehicle The liquid solution of a coating (containing the solvent and resins), which dries upon exposure to air.

Viscosity The thickness of a fluid or coating.

Volatile organic compound (VOC) Indicates substances that become hazardous upon vaporization, including xylene, toluene, and methanol. Measured in grams per liter or lb. per gallon.

Wallboard Also called drywall or Sheetrock.

Weathering The cumulative effects of sunlight and moisture on an exterior coating.

Wet edge The leading edge of a wet coating that remains workable. Critical for blending strokes.

Wrinkling A leathery texture in a new coating, caused by painting over a soft undercoat, coating a surface that is too hot or too cold, or applying too thick of a coat.

Yellowing An amber cast in a clear or light-colored coating. Most common with oil-based coatings. Exterior coatings also will yellow if used indoors.

RESOURCES

All 800 numbers are customer service numbers unless otherwise indicated.

PAINT COMPANIES

Benjamin Moore Paints
Montvale, NJ 07645
(201) 573-9600
(interior and exterior paints, primers, finishes)

Bruning Paint Co.
601 S. Haven St.
Baltimore, MD 21224
(800) 852-3636
(Synthetic Low-Odor Stain Killing Primer)

Carver Tripp
Parks Corp., Dept. FH
Somerset, MA 02726
(508) 679-5938
(water-based polyurethane finishes)

Deft
411 E. Keystone Ave.
Alliance, OH 44601-0476
(Deftoil Danish oil finish, Step Saver, exterior wood finish, satin finishing wax)

The Flood Co.
Dept. TFH
P.O. Box 399
Hudson, OH 44236-0399
(800) 321-3444
(Floetrol, Penetrol, Emulsabond, CWF and CWF-UV exterior finishes)

Kop-Coat, Inc.
K1834 Koppers Bldg.
Pittsburgh, PA 15219
(Wolman deck care products, including stain, brightener, water repellent, wood preservative)

McCloskey Products
1191 South Wheeling Road
Wheeling, IL 60090
(Ultra and Man O' War spar varnishes, Outdoor varnish, PolyureStain, Tungseal wood stain)

Messmer's, Inc.
P.O. Box 8
West Jordan, UT 84084
(801) 569-2426
(exterior seals and finishes)

Minwax
50 Chestnut Ridge Road
Montvale, NJ 07645
(800) 228-4722
(interior stains and finishes)

PPG Architectural Finishes Inc.
One PPG Place
Pittsburgh, PA 15272
Customer Communications Center and Tech Line: (800) 441-9695
Internet site: www.ppgaf.com
Emergency response: U.S.: (304) 843-1300; Canada: (514) 645-1320
Waste disposal: (412) 492-5481
(Pittsburgh Paints, primers, finishes, paint brushes; Olympic stains, sealers, wood restorers and cleaners)

Pratt & Lambert
M. L. Campbell
P.O. Box 22
Buffalo, NY 14240-0022
(800) 289-7728
(interior and exterior primers, paints, finishes, paint brushes; interior stains)

Rustoleum Corp.
11 Hawthorne Parkway
Vernon Hills, OH 60061
(Rust Reformer, rust stripper, primers, protective enamels, metallic colors)

Samuel Cabot, Inc.
100 Hale St.
Newburyport, MA 01950
(508) 465-1900
(exterior stains, wood brightener, wood cleaner)

Sherwin Williams Co.
Cleveland, OH 44101
Public relations: (216) 623-1511
Cuprinol Group: (800) 424-5837
(interior and exterior primers, paints, finishes, paint brushes, sprayers)

UGL
P.O. Box 70
Scranton, PA 18501
(800) 272-3235
(ZAR stains, finishes, paint and varnish remover)

William Zinsser & Co., Inc.
39 Belmont Dr.
Somerset, NJ 08875
(908) 469-8100
(Zinsser primer/sealers)

Wood Kote
P.O. Box 17192
Portland, OR 97217
(503) 285-8371
(wood finishes, gel stains, sealers)

Zehrung Corp.
16416 S.W. 72nd Ave.
Portland, OR 97224
(503) 684-3836
(primers, lacquer aerosol spray)

Natural Paints
AFM Enterprises
1140 Stacy Court
Riverside, CA 92507
(714) 781-6861

Auro Paints
(imported by) Sinan Co.
P.O. Box 857
Davis, CA 95617
(916) 753-3104

Livos Paints
2641 Cerrillos Road
Santa Fe, NM 87501
(505) 988-9111

Moser's Old-Fashioned Milk Paint
c/o Woodworker's Supply
1108 North Glen Road
Casper, WY 82601
(800) 645-9292

Old Fashioned Milk Paint Co.
P.O. Box 222
Groton, MA 01450
(617) 448-6336

Natural paint references provided by Debra Lynn Dadd, author of *Nontoxic and Natural*, published by Earthwise, 1525 New Hampshire Ave. N.W., Washington, DC 20036

PATCHING AND REPAIR

Abatron, Inc.
5501 95th Ave., Dept. FH
Kenosha, WI 53144
(800) 445-1754
(Liquid Wood and Woodepox wood restoration system)

Darworth Co.
Salisbury, CT 06070
(203) 843-1200
(Fix wood patch)

Donald Durham Co.
Des Moines, IA 50304
(515) 243-0491
(Durham's Rock Hard putty)

Homax Corp.
1610 6th St.
Bellingham, WA 98225
(205) 733-9029
(ceiling and wall texture, texture guns, wall patch)

Thoro System Products
7800 N.W. 38th St.
Miami, FL 33168
(305) 592-2081
(Thoropatch, Thorocrete masonry repair)

W. R. Bonsal Co.
Charlotte, NC 28224
(704) 525-1621
(Bonsal concrete acrylic binder)

PAINTER'S TAPE

3M Construction Markets Division
3M Center, 225-4S-08
P.O. Box 33225
St. Paul, MN 55133-3225
(800) 480-1704
Customer Service: 3M DYI Division
P.O. Box 33053
St. Paul, MN 55133-3053

Tape Specialties, Ltd.
Concord, Ontario L4K 1J5
(Painter's Mate masking tape)

PAINT STRIPPERS AND WOOD CLEANERS

Bio-Wash Wood Restoration Products, Inc.
10650 Country Road 81
Maple Grove, MN 55369
(800) 858-5011
(wood cleaners and restorers)

Bix Manufacturing Co., Inc.
P.O. Box 69
Ashland City, TN 37035
(203) 743-3263
(Bix stripper)

Dumond Chemicals, Inc.
New York, NY 10036
(212) 869-6350
(Peel-Away paint removal systems)

Okon
6000 North 13th Ave.
Lakewood, CO 80214
(303) 232-3571
(800) 237-0565
(wood cleaners and restorers, concrete and masonry sealers and stains)

Specialty Environmental Technologies, Inc.
4520 Glenmeade Lane
Auburn Hills, MI 48326
(800) 899-0401
(Citristrip)

W. M. Barr & Co.
Klean-Strip Division
(800) 238-2672
(Klean-Strip solvents, thinners, paint and varnish removers)

CAULK AND SPACKLE

Ace Hardware Corp.
2200 Kensington Court
Oak Brook, IL 60521
(800) 455-4223
(caulk, spackle, paint, tools, accessories)

Bondex International, Inc.
3616 Scarlet Oak Blvd.
St. Louis, MO 63122

Dap
Dayton, OH 45401
(937) 667-4461

Dripless, Inc.
52 Mission Circle, Suite 210
Santa Rosa, CA 95409
(707) 963-1773
(Dripless caulk guns)

Muralo Co.
Bayonne, NJ 07002
(the original Spackle)

Red Devil, Inc.
Union, NJ 07083-1933
(800) 247-3790

White Lightning Products Corp.
Atlanta, GA 30310
(206) 881-5770

MASONRY SEALERS

FLR Paints, Inc.
101 Prospect Ave.
Cleveland, OH 44115
(800) 867-8246
(H & C concrete and masonry stain)

Okon
(see under "Paint Strippers and Wood Cleaners")

UGL
(see under "Paint Companies")

BRUSHES AND ROLLERS

Bestt Liebco
1201 Jackson St.
Philadelphia, PA 19148
(800) 523-9095

Mr. Longarm
400 Walnut St.
P.O. Box 377
Greenwood, MO 64034-0377
(800) 821-3508
(extension poles, corner pads, edgers)

Maryland Brush Co.
3221 Frederick Ave.
Baltimore, MD 21229
(800) 654-0774

Paint Brush Corp.
P.O. Box 371
Vermillion, SD 57069-0371
(800) 843-9930
FAX (605) 624-6909

Purdy Paint Brushes
Portland, OR 97283-0097
(503) 286-8217

Sherwin Williams
(see under "Paint Companies")

Shur Line
Lancaster, NY 14086
(716) 683-2500
(painting accessories, edgers, etc.)

Wooster Brush Co.
Wooster, OH 44691
(216) 264-4440
(also offers roller covers)

SPRAYERS

Graco
P.O. Box 1441
Minneapolis, MN 55440
(612) 623-6737

Paint Trix Spray Tools
Sunnyvale, CA 94088
(408) 733-1052
(Scroller, Tra-Cut airless spray accessories)

Precision Valve Corp.
Preval Sprayer Division
P.O. Box 309
Yonkers, NY 10702
(914) 968-6500
(16 oz. portable sprayer)

Sherwin Williams
(see under "Paint Companies")

Wagner Spray Tech Corp.
1770 Fernbrook Lane
Plymouth, MN 55447
(800) 328-8251

SCRAPERS

Hyde Tools
54 Eastford Rd.
Southbridge, MA 01550
(800) 872-4933

Red Devil
(see under "Caulk and Spackle")

Sandvik Saws and Tools
P.O. Box 2036
Scranton, PA 18501
(717) 341-9500

Warner Manufacturing
Minneapolis, MN 55441
(612) 559-4740

PAINT CLEANERS

Advanced Developments, Inc.
San Diego, CA 92169
(800) 346-1633
(Mostenbocker's Lift Off grafitti remover)

Atlanta Sundries
Guardsman Products
Consumer Products Division
Grand Rapids, MI 49546
(616) 452-5181
(Goof-Off solvent and water-based all-purpose cleaners)

INZ Paint Clean Up
P.O. Box 905
Bozeman, MT 59771
(406) 586-6639
(for solvent-based coatings)

LADDERS

Werner
93 Werner Road
Greenville, PA 16125-9499
(800) 221-7307

Wing Enterprises
P.O. Box 3100
Springville, UT 84663-3100
(800) 453-1192
(Little Giant ladders)

PRE-PAINTED SIDING

International Paper
Masonite Division
One South Wacker Dr.
Chicago, IL 60606
(800) 223-1268
(Colorlok siding)

BOOKS

Pittsburgh Paints' Product & Painting Guide
(see under "Paint Companies")

Pratt & Lambert Specifications and Product Catalog
(see under "Paint Companies")

Sherwin Williams's Painting & Coating Systems
(see under "Paint Companies")

The Pittsburgh Paints guide refers to the following three books for causes of paint failure:

Diagnosing Paint Problems and Correcting Them
by Neil Garlock
Available from: The American Paint Journal Co.
2911 Washington Ave.
St. Louis, MO 63103

Craftsman's Manual and Textbook
Available from: Painting and Decorating Contractors of America
7223 Lee Highway
Falls Church, VA 22046

Paint Problem Solver
Available from: National Decoration Products Association
9334 Dielman Industrial Dr.
St. Louis, MO 63132

INDEX

DRYWALL: PROFESSIONAL TECHNIQUES FOR WALLS & CEILINGS

by Myron R. Ferguson

Installing drywall is one of the basic skills you need to master to create great-looking rooms. In this illustrated book, long-time drywall contractor Myron Ferguson shares the tips and techniques he uses to create beautifully smooth walls and ceilings. Inside, he demonstrates how to estimate and order drywall for any job, how to fit panels into odd shapes and spaces, how to tape and sand seams, how to create interesting wall textures, and more.

144 pages, paperback, $19.95 ISBN: 1-56158-133-X

Video also available

DRYWALL: HANGING AND TAPING

In this 60-minute companion video, Myron Ferguson demonstrates the tips and techniques that he uses to create smooth walls and ceilings.

VHS video, $19.95 ISBN: 1-56158-128-3

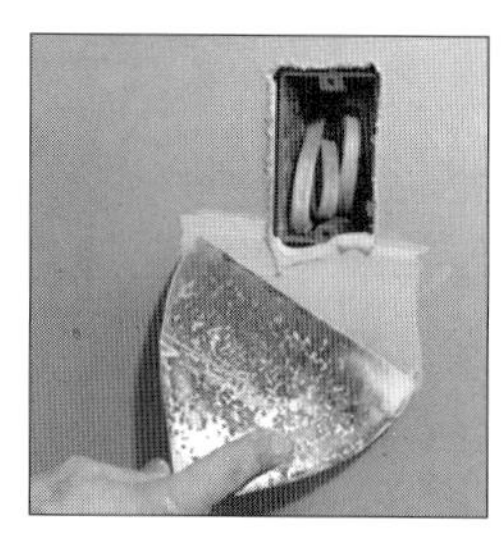

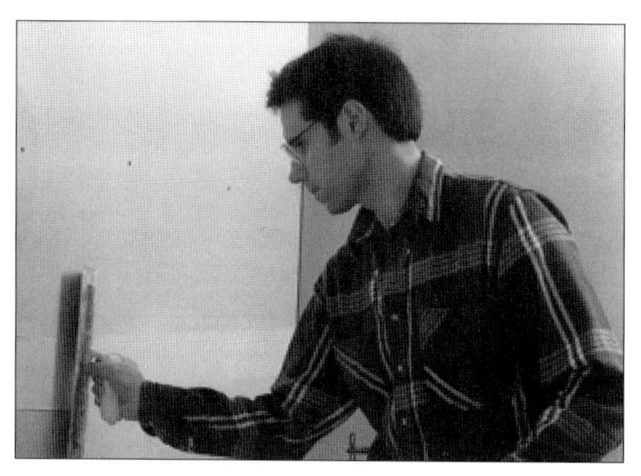

Many other titles are also available. You can find *Fine Homebuilding* books at bookstores everywhere, or order them direct from The Taunton Press by calling (800) 888-8286.

If you need to get professional results, add these books to your library.

SAFE HOME WIRING PROJECTS

by Rex Cauldwell

Detailed information on how to complete more than two dozen common household-wiring tasks. Includes wiring a kitchen disposal to a ceiling fan, security lights, and home entertainment systems. An emphasis on safety and how to find and buy safe and durable electrical components and fixtures make this book a must for any home electrician.

Paperback, $19.95 ISBN: 1-56158-164-X

MAKING PLASTIC-LAMINATE COUNTERTOPS

by Herrick Kimball

Here is a must-have book for anyone looking for sound practical information about the most economical type of countertops. Includes information about custom touches, such as wood edges and tile backsplashes.

Paperback, $19.95 ISBN: 1-56158-135-6

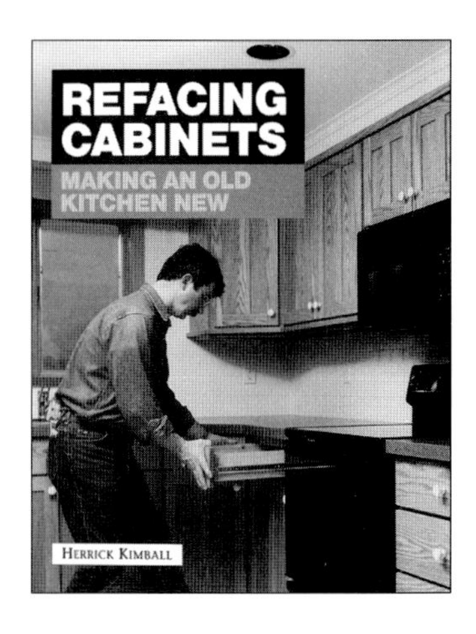

REFACING CABINETS
MAKING AN OLD KITCHEN NEW

(available December 1997)

by Herrick Kimball

By refacing old cabinets with new doors and real wood laminate, virtually anyone with basic woodworking skills can make a kitchen look new at a fraction of the cost of installing new cabinets. Professional remodeler Kimball shows readers everything they need to know to achieve stunning results. Detailed illustrations show every step in the process.

Paperback, $19.95 ISBN: 1-56158-128-3

PUBLISHER: **Jon Miller**

ACQUISITIONS EDITOR: **Julie Trelstad**

ASSISTANT EDITOR: **Karen Liljedahl**

EDITOR: **Ruth Hamel**

LAYOUT ARTIST: **Ken Swain**

PHOTOGRAPHER: **Mark Dixon**

INDEXER: **Tom McKenna**

TYPEFACE: **Frutiger Light**

PAPER: **70-lb. Mead Moistrite Matte**

PRINTER: **Quebecor Printing/Hawkins, Church Hill, Tennessee**